Mastering Azure API Management

A Practical Approach to Designing and Implementing an API-Centric Enterprise Architecture

Sven Malvik

Apress®

Mastering Azure API Management: A Practical Approach to Designing and Implementing an API-Centric Enterprise Architecture

Sven Malvik
Fjerdingby, Norway

ISBN-13 (pbk): 978-1-4842-8010-2
https://doi.org/10.1007/978-1-4842-8011-9

ISBN-13 (electronic): 978-1-4842-8011-9

Managing Director, Apress Media LLC: Welmoed Spahr
Acquisitions Editor: Joan Murray
Development Editor: Laura Berendson
Coordinating Editor: Jill Balzano

Cover image designed by Freepik (www.freepik.com)

Distributed to the book trade worldwide by Springer Science+Business Media LLC, 1 New York Plaza, Suite 4600, New York, NY 10004. Phone 1-800-SPRINGER, fax (201) 348-4505, e-mail orders-ny@springer-sbm.com, or visit www.springeronline.com. Apress Media, LLC is a California LLC and the sole member (owner) is Springer Science + Business Media Finance Inc (SSBM Finance Inc). SSBM Finance Inc is a **Delaware** corporation.

For information on translations, please e-mail booktranslations@springernature.com; for reprint, paperback, or audio rights, please e-mail bookpermissions@springernature.com.

Apress titles may be purchased in bulk for academic, corporate, or promotional use. eBook versions and licenses are also available for most titles. For more information, reference our Print and eBook Bulk Sales web page at http://www.apress.com/bulk-sales.

Printed on acid-free paper

Hi boys, Even and Emil.

Table of Contents

About the Author

 **Sven Malvik** is an experienced Azure expert. He specializes in compliancy and digital transformation, most recently in the financial industry. He has decades of experience in software development, DevOps, and cloud engineering. Sven is a Microsoft MVP in Azure and a speaker, presenting sessions and tutorials at a number of global conferences, user group meetings, and international companies.

About the Technical Reviewer

 **Martin Ehrnst** is a speaker and technical writer within Azure and surrounding Microsoft-related technologies. With 15 years of experience in the IT industry, he has gained significant competency from working with countless customers and technical implementations around the globe. He believes sharing knowledge is key to success internally and for the broader community. A recognized Microsoft MVP in Azure since 2019, he holds several technology certifications.

Acknowledgments

Thank you so much Nina, my awesome wife and friend for over 26 years. When I first asked you whether I should sign the contract for this book, you said "You should sign," and I signed. You never doubted that I would write this book. When I hadn't written for some days, you carefully reminded me without putting any pressure on me, so I never felt any pressure. Many evenings when I was behind my desk writing this book being selfish in a way, you took care of our boys, made dinner, and walked our dog. I love you!

I want to also thank Vipps AS, my employer, for being so supportive of this endeavor and especially my manager Kristian Skønberg Løvik. You started all this when you first asked me if I would like to speak at Microsoft Build and talk about our journey with Azure API Management. You made this book happen in the first place and always supported me on the way.

Finally, I thank all who I have been working together with. You helped me to get where I am today: Helge Tesdal, Evgeny Borzenin, Per Reidar Bøhler, Maxim Salnikov, and Miao Jiang.

Foreword

Over the course of my technical career, and as a full-stack developer, I have dedicated many years to building web applications. I learned that when we developers manage multiple parts of a solution, the need for a well-architected, precisely implemented, tested, and documented API is crucial. It is the "glue" for the application components or even for the multiple heterogeneous applications. I recognized that the closer you get to the launch date, you have to have solutions for API security, performance, scalability, reliability, and monitoring. Multiply it by the number of APIs in the project, add support for the cloud and on-premise target environments, onboard new developer teams (sometimes external, with limited access) - and the need for a solid API management solution becomes crystal clear. I learned to understand and respect API layer complexity far beyond the requirement for having a well-architected "communication" protocol.

I met Sven Malvik, the author of this book, for the first time a few years ago at a developer community meetup I hosted at the Microsoft office in Norway. We got talking and I was shocked when he mentioned how many APIs he and his team support and add on monthly basis to Vipps (Norway's largest mobile payment provider, and an ecosystem where Sven leads Cloud Platform). Knowing that Vipps runs on Azure, I immediately thought, this level of knowledge and expertise with Azure API Management service should be shared with the developer community! And now my hopes have been realized. Sven is a natural-born technical communicator, trainer, and community organizer who is extremely passionate about sharing his Azure cloud experience with the developers. He was a guest (presenting on Azure API Management) on my video show "Cloud Stories from Norway," and with great pleasure, I nominated and guided Sven on his way to becoming a Microsoft MVP.

Fast-forward to today. After our countless joint events and collaborations focused on the technical audience, Sven kindly invited me to write the foreword to his book, *Mastering Azure API Management*. It is a culmination of his aspirations to share proven knowledge and expertise with the goal of teaching developers how to efficiently build great solutions.

From the very first chapter, you dive deep into the technical demos, examples, and expert how-to guidance. And it's reassuring to know that everything you learn from this book is based on Sven's experience with building the enormous scale ecosystem reliably serving millions of the users in Nordics every day. All of his findings, recommendations, and insights about Azure API Management are 100% real world!

Skills in Azure API Management service provide a strong foundation for cloud developers. It allows them to build projects faster and better, use fewer resources on management after the proper initial setup, and be ready for future innovations in cloud technologies. I recommend you read this book and keep it on your desk. You will revisit particular chapters during the building of your API management strategy for your current and future projects.

Enjoy reading and learning from Sven!

Maxim Salnikov

Azure Developer Engagement Lead at Microsoft

Technical Communities Organizer

Keynote Speaker

December 2021

Introduction

Have you ever tried to program in two languages at the same time? When I started working with Azure API Management, I learned about the concept of policies, which happens to be XML files with C# code statements. Many API developers and administrators struggle with policies because of that but also because of its enormous power.

Many engineers that I helped to understand Azure API Management in conversations and during workshops experience this Azure service as a smarter reverse proxy compared to other services such as Azure Application Gateway and Azure Front Door. However, they find it somehow hard to grasp the details of it such as how products and subscriptions fit into APIs or when, where, and how to develop policies. Others look for ways to integrate Azure API Management into an existing architecture, be it hybrid or cloud native, and want to ensure secure end-to-end communication between API consumers and API backend web services.

This book will help you to understand why Azure API Management is more than a reverse proxy but a service for managing an API-centric enterprise architecture. You will learn about its core concepts and how you can work with them in a productive way such as publishing APIs, creating API versions, and developing policies. You will also dive into setting up a developer portal for your users, the API consumers, that they can use to learn about your APIs and subscribe to them so they can call an API while the API backend web service is protected in a secure way. If you are an administrator or architect, this book will teach you different networking modes so you can integrate Azure API Management into your hybrid or cloud native architecture. You will then learn how to log and monitor the traffic that is going through Azure API Management besides other typical administration tasks such as automatic backups and caching.

I have worked with Azure API Management since 2018. As I was the responsible engineer for Azure API Management in the company I work for, I made API deployments simpler for our developers than they often are described in blog posts. Microsoft liked the approach and invited me to Microsoft Build to talk about our journey. I have written this book to teach you Azure API Management in detail and everything that's important to integrate it into your architecture, so you won't need to read endless blog posts and spend hundreds of hours in testing everything out. Have fun!

PART I

Getting Started

CHAPTER 1

Quick Start

Let's get right down to business and have some fun in the meantime. In this first chapter, we will focus on getting you onboard and up to speed with Azure API Management as quickly as possible, so that you can get the most out of it.

In this chapter, you will learn how to provision API Management from the Azure portal and then add a first API that you will try out directly from the API Management portal.

In order to get started, you will need an Azure account. If you already have an Azure account and a subscription that you can create resources in, then great! Feel free to skip the following section and head directly to the section on provisioning Azure API Management.

Create an Azure Account

If you are new to Azure or just want to have your own Azure account other than the one you may use at work, this section will help you to get started. If you already have an Azure account, feel free to skip this section and sign in to the Azure portal directly.

Azure provides students with a credit for creating a free *Azure for Students* account. The amount of the credit may vary from country to country. You find all details on the following website: `https://azure.microsoft.com/en-us/free/students/`.

Please visit the Azure website `https://azure.microsoft.com/en-us/free/` and sign in with your Microsoft credentials. In case you don't have a Microsoft account yet, follow the instructions for creating one. A Microsoft account is free of charge.

Once you have signed in with your Microsoft credentials, you will be presented with a form for creating an Azure account. Besides your name and email address, Microsoft will ask you to identify yourself by phone and by card. There is no charge involved. Microsoft just wants to verify your identity.

© Sven Malvik 2022

S. Malvik, *Mastering Azure API Management*, https://doi.org/10.1007/978-1-4842-8011-9_1

After having signed up for an Azure account, you can sign in to the Azure portal where you can find a pay-as-you-go subscription. An Azure subscription logically associates your user account and the resources that you will create.

Once you have an Azure account, you can start using its services. New Azure accounts start with 12 months of some free services. You will find more information on the Azure website.

Note   You started a 12-month free trial of Azure. However, Azure API Management is not free of charge and you will still be paying for this service depending on the pricing tier.

You might be discouraged now knowing that you can't try Azure API Management without spending money. Let me assure you that there is a pricing tier that will work without spending money. We will discuss this in more detail in the next section.

Provision Azure API Management

Now let's provision an API Management resource. You have plenty of options and technologies to choose from when it comes to managing Azure resources, including Azure Bicep, Azure PowerShell, and Azure CLI, just to name a few. We will work in the Azure portal which, in my opinion, is the simplest way to get started to learn Azure API Management.

Before we begin though, I want to briefly mention costs before you actually create an Azure resource so you won't be surprised later, but also understand when you might have to pay for Azure API Management. In the previous section, we created a free Azure account. However, Azure API Management is not a free service, which means that at some point you will have to choose the optimal pricing tier in order to minimize costs. Fortunately, there is one pricing tier called **Consumption** that has some free calls per month before users get charged. This can of course change over time, and so I recommend checking the documentation about API Management pricing.

If you have skipped the previous section about creating an Azure account and haven't signed into the Azure portal yet, please do so by visiting the following address: https://portal.azure.com/.

Figure 1-1 shows how to create an API Management resource from the Azure portal. Click "Create a resource" on the left side, and search in the list of all Azure resources for "API Management." Once the service appears in the result list, select it, and you will be presented the API Management resource. Click now on "Create" for configuring your API Management resource.

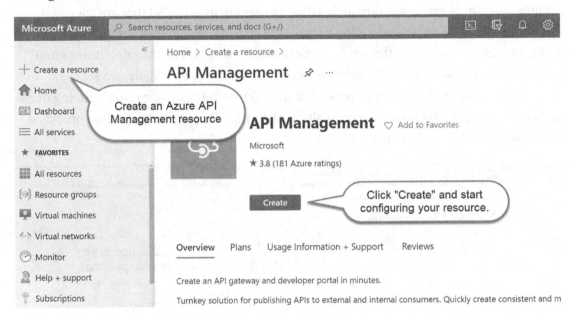

Figure 1-1. *Creating an API Management resource*

We will now configure our first API Management resource. The configuration of API Management is split into multiple tabs, "Basics," "Monitoring," "Scale," "Managed Identity," "Virtual network," "Protocol settings," and "Tags." If you are not familiar with Azure yet, you might find this overwhelming. Be assured that we will discuss every corner of API Management throughout this book. In this chapter, we will focus on the first tab of the configuration, "Basics."

The first four fields of the basic configuration of an API Management resource are common for almost all resources in Azure. That is the subscription this resource shall be associated with in case you got more than one. If you are not familiar with Azure subscriptions, please read the previous section where we created a new Azure account. The seconds field describes the resource group that you want to put this resource in. It serves as a logical container for all resources that may share the same lifecycle. In the third field, you will set the region where you want this resource to be provisioned in. I set it to "West Europe" where I live, so API calls would have a shorter distance to travel and probably be quicker than if I had chosen the United States or Asia. The last field is the resource name. The name of an API Management resource must be unique and can't be changed later as it serves as part of the domain that you will need to access the service.

Figure 1-2 shows the basic configuration of an API Management resource where you can see the four configurations that are common for almost all Azure resources. Additionally, there are three more fields that we need to look at and that are special to API Management. The "Organization name" is used in several places, including the title of the developer portal and the sender of notification emails. The "Administrator email" is the email address to which all notification emails will be sent. Finally, we set the "Pricing tier." I have already mentioned that we will use the "Consumption" pricing tier in this chapter as it gives us some free calls. It also suits our purpose of getting quickly a high-level overview of API Management.

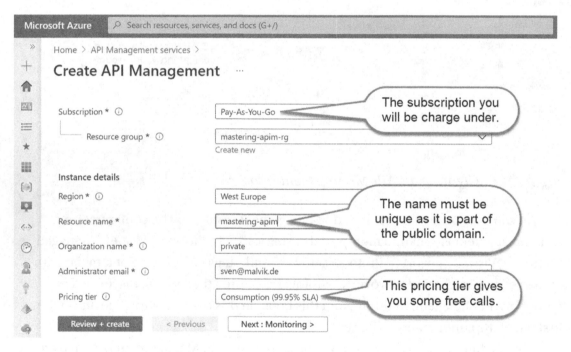

Figure 1-2. *Configuring the basics*

We will skip the remaining configuration tabs for now, so click directly on "Review + create" at the bottom. This step will verify all your input fields. In case you forgot to set a field, it will be highlighted with an error message. Once all fields are set correctly, you can continue by clicking "Create." The process of provisioning API Management with the "Consumption" pricing tier takes about 2 minutes. Once the deployment is complete, please click the "Go to resource" button for visiting the overview dashboard of API Management. You will also find your newly created resource inside the deployed resource group.

Add API

Now that we have an API Management resource up and running, we will continue and add a first API. If you haven't navigated to your API Management resource yet, please do so now. You can also search for the resource name in the upper search bar in the Azure portal.

Your API Management resource will look similar to mine that is shown in Figure 1-3. It shows the overview of the resource with all of the essentials that we provided during the basic configuration in the previous section about creating an API Management resource. Click in the menu on the left side on "APIs" for adding a new API.

Figure 1-3. *Overview of API Management dashboard*

Figure 1-4 shows multiple options of adding an API. We will discuss all of them in detail in the following chapter. For now, we will focus on the OpenAPI specification, formerly known as Swagger specification. It is an API description format for REST APIs. Click "OpenAPI" for adding a REST API.

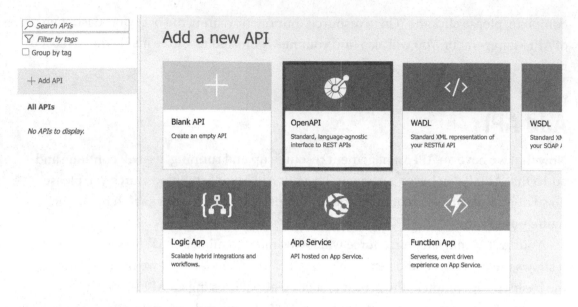

Figure 1-4. *Adding new API*

We won't create an API from scratch here as it is not the focus of this book. Instead, we will add an existing backend API to API Management by importing the public available "Demo Conference API," which is provided by Microsoft and hosted in Azure. This API Management API will become a façade for the backend API.

Figure 1-5 shows the configuration for creating an API from an OpenAPI specification, where we can set the URL of the Demo Conference API. The following two fields, "Display name" and "Name," will be automatically extracted from the specification once the URL is set. The only remaining information we will need is the context path under which we want to make this API available for the users. In this example, I set the field "API URL suffix" to "conferenceapi," so the base URL of this API will become `https://mastering-api-management.azure-api.net/conferenceapi`. You should now be able to click "Create" for adding API to your API Management resource.

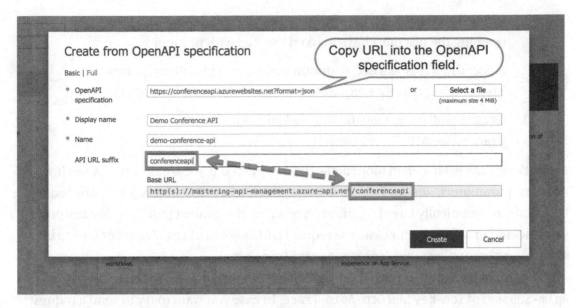

Figure 1-5. *Create API from OpenAPI specification*

Congratulations! You have just added your first API to API Management. You should see "Demo Conference API" in the list of all APIs on the left side of Figure 1-4. In the next section, we will test one endpoint from the API Management portal and from the local machine using cURL.

Test API

We are finally ready to test the new API. There are several options to choose from: the local machine using cURL, PowerShell, Postman or Visual Studio Code plugin, and from the API Management portal directly. To get you onboarded and to bring you up to speed as quickly as possible, I suggest continuing in the API Management portal and call our new API directly from there.

API Management Portal

Figure 1-6 shows the three steps we will go through to test the "Demo Conference API." I will first mention all three steps before I will go into the details and explain what we see on the right side.

1. Click "Test" in the top menu of the "Demo Conference API" for opening the test tab. I have marked the step with number 1.

2. Select the "GetSpeakers" endpoint in the list of all API endpoints. This endpoint doesn't require any parameters and is easy to test.

3. Click "Send" for calling the API backend of the Demo Conference API.

Let's discuss each step in more detail. In the "Test" tab, we create a call by setting headers, parameters, and body, in case we would send a POST http request. The request URL is set automatically based on the service name, the context path, and the endpoint you selected in step 2. In our case, the request URL is set to `https://mastering-api-management.azure-api.net/conferenceapi/speakers`.

You might have noticed that there are already set two headers in the request, `Ocp-Apim-Subscription-Key` and `Ocp-Apim-Trace`. In case you want to try to send a request from outside the API Management portal, that is, with cURL, you will need the first header which is a subscription key. We will discuss API Management subscriptions and subscription keys in a later chapter.

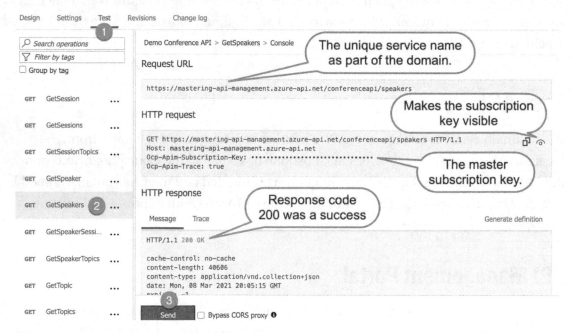

Figure 1-6. *Testing Demo Conference API*

We have seen how we can use the API Management portal to test an API in its simplest way. It's a good way of quickly checking whether an API works or not.

Command Line

Another option for testing an API quickly is by sending the request from the command line by using cURL. We have seen in our example that we need a subscription key to access this API. Click the eye icon you can see in Figure 1-6 and copy the entire header `Ocp-Apim-Subscription-Key: <SUBSCRIPTION KEY>`.

Listing 1-1 shows the cURL command for accessing the same endpoint as in our previous example. Remember that the service name is unique. You will have created your service with a different service name, so please make sure to replace both the *subscription key* and the *service name*.

Listing 1-1. Calling an API Management endpoint with cURL

```
curl -H "Ocp-Apim-Subscription-Key: <SUBSCRIPTION KEY>" -X GET \
https://<SERVICE NAME>.azure-api.net/conferenceapi/speakers
```

Summary

In this chapter, you learned about a core element of Azure API Management. Congratulations, you now understand how to add an API and then call it directly from the API Management portal and from your local machine using cURL. In the next chapter, we will discuss what it is that makes API Management so powerful by discussing today's challenges and how API Management addresses them.

CHAPTER 2

Overview

Before we dive into the details of Azure API Management and learn how to integrate this service into an organization, let's take a step back and talk about the value of having an enterprise API platform. A typical use case of Azure API Management in organizations is to make digital assets available that otherwise would be hidden in legacy systems. Another example of why you would want to use Azure API Management in your organization is the possibility to create new products by bundling APIs from different systems into one common accessible unit.

In the first part of this chapter, I want to briefly highlight why APIs are the biggest differentiator for success and give you some examples. Once you understand what makes APIs so powerful, we will discuss them in more detail and learn the basics of web APIs. Finally, you will learn how to manage web APIs with an enterprise API platform and take a look at Azure API Management by discussing its core components.

Unlocking Digital Assets with APIs

In the 2021 Connectivity Benchmark Report published by MuleSoft, 800 global IT leaders were asked about the state of connectivity and digital transformation. It states that an average enterprise has about 900 applications, whereas only a third of those applications are integrated together, making it very difficult for organizations to deliver a connected experience. Digital assets are locked in hundreds of systems making organizations slow to innovate and being agile.

The demand from business for integration projects is increasing. The ability to unlock, analyze, and act on data has become foundational to growth.

IT leaders report that integration via APIs is critical to their digital transformation strategy. Well-designed APIs add new possibilities like controlling access to digital assets, combining legacy applications with new applications, and empowering professional developers and citizen developers to experiment, innovate, and react to changing customer needs.

13

© Sven Malvik 2022
S. Malvik, *Mastering Azure API Management*, https://doi.org/10.1007/978-1-4842-8011-9_2

APIs let developers access and combine systems, even if those systems were never intended to interoperate. One developer may use an API to look up customer data for a new application, while another developer is using the same API for adding a new feature to another application. Connectivity via APIs is not only a critical enabler of digital transformation but also the biggest differentiator of success. Let me illustrate through the following three examples from three different industries.

Payments

Vipps is a Norwegian payment service that provides an app to its four million users for ordering items online, making purchases in stores, and splitting up lunch checks with friends. It lets users pay invoices across almost every bank in Norway directly in the Vipps app. Considering Norway's population of about 5.3 million, this app is used by three out of four people and makes Vipps a critical part of the financial infrastructure in Norway.

Norwegian's love Vipps because it simplifies the way they do payments. Especially during the pandemic, partners and merchants can easily adopt Vipps and let their customers do financial transactions in a very convenient way. It follows an API strategy that lets partners, merchants, and its own developers easily use Vipps' services.

Initially, it migrated its application infrastructure directly to virtual machines in Azure. To upgrade its data structure and get the most out of Azure services, it also migrated from Oracle to Azure SQL Database. It then began using Azure API Management to publish Vipps microservices to internal developers along with partners and merchants. Today, Vipps builds new services using these APIs in API Management, like the Vipps "Mobilapponnement," which is a cell phone plan which Vipps' users can order directly in the app. This new product was built in a very short amount of time and has become a great success. That's the power of APIs.

Manufacturing

ZEISS is a German manufacturer and international leader in the fields of optical systems and optoelectronics. ZEISS maintained a 20-year-old back-end system with hard-coded business rules. Its developers couldn't easily update, reroute, or track orders without reconfiguring the system. Changes were very costly and time-consuming. ZEISS needed a more agile order management and processing system. They started to follow an API-strategy and started to decouple front-end interfaces from back-end systems. They also wanted to go global and distribute the order-processing environment across multiple Azure datacenters to provide faster service to customers around the world. Azure API Management serves as the gateway to the regional resources, giving ZEISS a single place for efficiently managing its APIs hosted on-premises and on Azure.

ZEISS customers benefit today from faster order fulfillment and timely notifications of progress, something the existing system couldn't do.

You can read the full technical story about Carl Zeiss AG on `https://customers.microsoft.com/en-us/story/1336089737047375040-zeiss-accelerates-cloud-first-development-on-azure-and-streamlines-order-processing`. Thanks for sharing Microsoft.

Automotive

Mercedes-Benz is a German automotive marque that has built over two million luxury and commercial passenger cars. The research and development teams jokingly call these passenger cars "Container-driven cars," as its microservices-based architecture relies on containers for updating the head unit computer in a car's dashboard. The head unit computer runs the infotainment system, navigation system, steering wheel audio control, handsfree calling system, parking system, and other apps. Until recently, this unit was designed as a monolith. Changes were time-consuming to implement as apps were developed by several development teams in North America and Germany.

The way they solved these challenges was to break the monolith into a microservice-based platform that is based on Azure Kubernetes Service (AKS). They use APIs for connecting apps, data, and back-end services, thus, decoupling back-end APIs from the microservices.

Microservices that one team is implementing can already be used by another team and vendors using APIs and by mocking back-end services that are being implemented. This approach enables all teams and vendors to build products together and simultaneously by sharing their APIs.

Thanks so much to Microsoft and Mercedes-Benz Research & Development North America for sharing this story. You can read the full technical story on `https://customers.microsoft.com/ja-jp/story/784791-mercedes-benz-r-and-d-creates-container-driven-cars-powered-by-microsoft-azure`

Understanding the Basics of web APIs

Throughout this book, we will learn how to manage an API-centric enterprise using Azure API Management as our enterprise API platform. Before we dive into the details of Azure API Management, we need to understand APIs.

API is the acronym for *A*pplication *P*rogramming *I*nterface which let applications communicate with each other by abstracting the underlying implementation and provide access to digital assets such as documents, pictures, or other digital content and to interact with logic such as turning on the lights in a smart home. A web API is an API over the Internet using the HTTP(S) protocol. As Azure API Management only supports HTTP(S), we will focus on web APIs in this book.

Web APIs can receive requests from web browsers, mobile applications, desktop applications, IoT, and also from back-end services that run in the cloud or on-premises. Some publicly available and popular web APIs are Google Map APIs, YouTube APIs, and Twitter APIs. Access to web APIs can also be restricted to internal systems only. Other web APIs are available also for partners.

A web API exposes endpoints that are digital locations to digital assets and logic. In Azure API Management, an API endpoint is represented by an API operation. When working with web APIs in the context of this book, there are two terms that are essential, *SOAP* and *REST*. Both describe how to access a web service and what operations they perform. Let us discuss them briefly in the following sections as they are both supported by Azure API Management.

SOAP

SOAP is an acronym and stands for *S*imple *O*bject *A*ccess *P*rotocol. It is an XML-based messaging protocol for exchanging information among computers over the Internet and is widely used by older APIs. SOAP enables client applications to connect to remote services and invoke remote methods. It is platform and operating system independent, so client and server applications that want to communicate with each other can be implemented in different programming languages and with different technologies using SOAP as an intermediate language. For example, a .NET application running on one computer can invoke a method in a Java application that is running on a different computer using the SOAP messaging protocol making it very lightweight to communicate. The functionality of a SOAP-based web service is described in a WSDL document.

WSDL

WSDL is also an acronym and stands for *Web Services Description Language*. It describes the contract between a web service and a client in XML-format. A client that connects to a web service will read its WSDL document to determine what functionality it exposes.

Listing 2-1 shows a fraction of a simple example of a WSDL document which is taken from the *WSDL document specification*. We see three main elements in this example. The first element `<message>` defines the data for an operation being communicated and is used to describe the data being exchanged between a web service and the client application. We see two messages, an input message for the request and an output message for the response. The second element, `<portType>`, defines a complete operation that is exposed by a web service and the messages that it involves. The third element, `<binding>`, defines the protocol and data format for each port type.

Listing 2-1. A simple WSDL document

```
<message name="getTermRequest">
  <part name="term" type="xs:string"/>
</message>

<message name="getTermResponse">
  <part name="value" type="xs:string"/>
</message>

<portType name="glossaryTerms">
  <operation name="getTerm">
    <input message="getTermRequest"/>
    <output message="getTermResponse"/>
  </operation>
</portType>

<binding type="glossaryTerms" name="b1">
  <soap:binding style="document"
  transport="http://schemas.xmlsoap.org/soap/http" />
```

```
<operation>
  <soap:operation soapAction="http://example.com/getTerm"/>
  <input><soap:body use="literal"/></input>
  <output><soap:body use="literal"/></output>
</operation>
</binding>
```

SOAP with WSDL is centered around passing documents. Requests and responses are typically very well structured, which makes it a great candidate for two parties that would need a very strict contract such as inter-bank communication. The downside of SOAP is its very verbose XML structure. However, SOAP was widely used some years ago and you will find it for older APIs. Today, most APIs use a RESTful approach that we will discuss in the following section.

REST

It was his call to defend the design choices to engineers from all over the world. Dr. Roy Thomas Fielding, an American computer scientist, had worked on the foundation of the World Wide Web, HTTP 1.1. Input came from distinguished engineers with decades of experience, and every detail had to be explained to them. It was a very important and challenging process. The result of many discussions was a model that led to some core principles that we now call REST (*RE*presentational *S*tate *T*ransfer). The principles of REST are as follows:

- **Client-server architecture**: Client and server are decoupled from each other and live in their own bounded contexts.

- **Statelessness**: The client is responsible for providing all information in all requests so that a server can understand the context as it doesn't store state.

- **Catchability**: The data in a response is required to be implicitly or explicitly labeled as cacheable or non-cacheable, so a client eventually reuses the data.

- **Layered system**: A request might go through other systems, such as a security system or load-balancing system, before it reaches the responding web service.

- **Code on demand**: A client's functionality can be extended to download and execute code from the server.

- **Uniform interface**: As all components follow the same constraints, it simplifies and decouples the interactions between them.

You might have noticed that REST is a software architectural style, not an implementation. It defines how web standards, such as HTTP and URI, are supposed to be used. We call web services that follow this architectural style as RESTful. Azure API Management supports two formats that describe RESTful web services, *WADL* and *OpenAPI*.

WADL

WADL means *W*eb *A*pplication *D*escription *L*anguage and describes a web service to its requesting clients. It defines a contract between a client and a server. A contract might not always be necessary. Development teams who work closely together and who can communicate clearly how a web service needs to be called and a response be interpreted might find introducing a contract with WADL as an unnecessary overhead. On the other hand, there might be one or many development teams who integrate complex enterprise systems with each other. It might also be the case that you need to integrate with a legacy system that is not actively maintained anymore. A strict contract makes it in such a case easier for all parties to communicate and integrate their systems with each other.

The WADL contract is an XML document that describes the resources of a web service that can be accessed by a client. Listing 2-2 shows a simple example of a WADL document which represents a resource for listing and adding books.

Listing 2-2. A simple WADL document

```
<application xmlns="http://wadl.dev.java.net/2009/02">
    <resources base="http://example.com/api">
        <resource path="books">
            <method name="GET"/>
            <method name="POST"/>
        </resource>
    </resources>
</application>
```

A WADL document is often used to create client-side code and it appeals therefore to developers that have a strong SOAP background where it is common to generate client-side code from a WSDL document.

It is not a widely adopted description language, as it is very time-consuming to describe a web service manually using this format. A simpler and more adopted format in the developer community is the OpenAPI specification that we will discuss in the following section.

OpenAPI

If you have developed and used RESTful APIs during your IT career, chances are that you already are familiar with the term "Swagger." Today, Swagger is a set of tools for implementing the OpenAPI specification. The name "OpenAPI" was actually donated in 2015. Before that, we called today's OpenAPI specification the Swagger specification. It is a very popular specification and open source format for describing and documenting modern RESTful APIs. While description languages such as WSDL and WADL describe web services in the XML format, OpenAPI documents are represented in either YAML or JSON, which makes these documents less verbose and more human-readable.

Listing 2-3 shows a simple OpenAPI document in the YAML format for listing cars. You may notice that this document includes descriptions which allow us to generate API documentations. It is very convenient for a developer to immediately know what this API and the endpoints are doing. It simplifies how we can integrate our systems with each other.

Listing 2-3. A simple OpenAPI document in the YAML format

```
openapi: 3.0.0
info:
  version: 1.0.0
  title: Simple car API
  description: A simple API for listing cars
paths:
  /cars:
    get:
      description: Returns a list of cars
      responses:
        '200':
          description: Successful response
```

Throughout the book, we generally use examples that are based on OpenAPI documents as these are the most common in today's organizations. However, there are scenarios where we have to integrate to older web APIs that are described in WSDL or WADL. The behavior of Azure API Management is the same, as we will see in a later chapter when we will import various web APIs.

HTTP Clients for Testing RESTful web APIs

We send a lot of requests to Azure API Management and we can test APIs directly from the Azure portal. However, this is not always practical when we develop our APIs on our local machine. We would need to switch back and forth from our local machine to the Azure portal whenever we want to test a change. There are two HTTP clients that I like very much and that I will use throughout this book, *cURL* and *Postman*.

cURL

cURL is an open source command-line tool that is well suited for sending HTTP requests. We have seen it in action in the example (Listing 1-1) where we called an API endpoint for listing all speakers of a demo conference API. It can be downloaded for almost any operating system and architecture. You can either download the sources and binary directly from the *curl website*, or you can follow the instructions for installing cURL on Linux, Windows, or Mac from the *curl documentation* pages.

Postman

The Postman app is another HTTP client that is a great tool for interacting with web APIs. It's an especially great tool for an author, as it makes it possible for me to share all the requests that I perform throughout the book with you. You can simply use the import feature, as highlighted in Figure 2-1.

Figure 2-1 demonstrates how to send a request with Postman to the same API operation as in the first chapter when testing the Demo Conference API. I set the URL for the API operation and the subscription key that I got from the Azure portal. As mentioned earlier, Postman allows for sharing of requests with its parameters and headers in the form of collections.

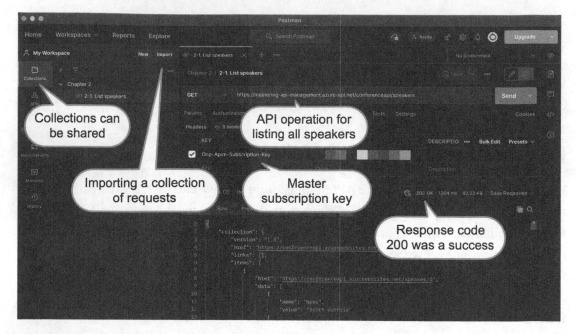

Figure 2-1. *Sending a simple request from Postman*

Enterprise API Platform in Essence

The center of an enterprise API platform is its consumable APIs. You might be already familiar with the API-first approach which talks about creating an API first before its implementation to ensure that its consumers get the best possible experience. Similar to this approach is the API as a product strategy which takes this one step further.

An API as a product strategy is a customer-oriented strategy that focuses on the demand of solving a digital problem rather than the supply of a digital asset. While it is true that a company's developers and partners benefit from having convenient access to digital assets, an enterprise API platform looks beyond.

As companies unlock their digital assets and make them accessible through web APIs, it is important to look at the overall experience across all web APIs from a developer's perspective for achieving the best possible adoption. A good developer experience is influenced by many factors such as consistent documentations, comprehensible capabilities, and common design guidelines. As these are important factors for creating successful API products, there are other important factors that need to be taken into account and that otherwise might lead to a bad experience. Among these factors are developer onboarding, user management, cost management, API security and governance, versioning and revisioning, performance, stability, scalability and resiliency, health monitoring, and a great DevOps experience.

We have briefly discussed the benefits of following an API as a product strategy and how an enterprise API platform takes this one step further. However, the following parts go into more detail and explain the main aspects of an enterprise API platform that are useful for understanding Azure API Management.

Consistent Documentation

One major success factor of an API is its documentation. Great API documentation can create a great developer experience. While this is an important ingredient for a successful API, it does not guarantee the success of an enterprise API platform. Such platforms host usually many different APIs that were developed by many different teams and many different people. Some of the APIs might even be several years old and either lack documentation completely or be inconsistent in their appearance and functionality because they were out of sync with the latest changes. A successful enterprise API platform delivers consistent documentations across all its hosted web APIs.

Comprehensible Capabilities

Comprehensible API capabilities that do not overlap are another important ingredient of a successful enterprise API platform. As an example, it might easily happen that two teams in an organization build each a web service that require user information as part of their services. As there is no user information web service available yet, one team decides to create a new user information web service along with the actual web service. The second team builds only one web service and integrated user information capabilities into it which they also exposed in the web API. There exist now three new web APIs where two of them expose the same user information capabilities. An API user who needs to access user information might find it difficult to choose between one of these two web APIs.

Common Design Guidelines

API design involves many aspects such as API governance, developer experience, performance, and, most important, a value proposition, to name a few. There are many constraints to take into account when designing an API. While all these aspects are important, an API user cares first and foremost about solving a problem that might require using several APIs. An enterprise API platform supports an API user by providing common design guidelines across all APIs it hosts. These users benefit from such an API platform as they do not have to learn and understand different API styles and instead experience an API platform that supports common design guidelines.

API User Onboarding

The main purpose of an enterprise API platform is to serve its API users with information and capabilities. To get API users to this point of using an API product and providing value to them, there are important steps to take first such as registering, finding the documentation, getting API keys, but also understanding code examples. A good way to help API users is to allow them to register instantly via a self-service and also providing them with everything necessary in one place so they do not need to search for what they need. An enterprise API platform such as Azure API Management provides a developer portal for this purpose, making it very simple for its API users to get started immediately and providing them with value.

User Management

Users of any platform must be managed. Resetting a password is just one example. In case of an enterprise API platform, there are additional examples and use cases such as reactivating or deactivating a user. A certain user might not work for a partner anymore, so this user does not have the same relation to your organization at this point. Another use case is where you might want to withdraw an API subscription key because a certain user might not be eligible to use a particular API product anymore. This can be the case when an API user did not pay its bill, which might be based on a monthly usage report that you generated through the API platform.

Health Monitoring

When a backend service is not responding in the same way as it is intended to, we must know about it quickly, so we can respond and mitigate a possible incident. An enterprise API platform is a façade to backend services and a great place to monitor the health of the backend services that are behind this façade. Response codes, response times, but also API's usage are all important measures that should be considered for monitoring. These data help not only to mitigate a problem more quickly, but also to learn from them, so improvements can be made before something unforeseen happens.

Governance and Compliance

APIs are the doors to capabilities and assets through web services. As these doors are supposed to be open for some developers and closed to others, APIs can expose considerable risk to an enterprise where it is undocumented or somehow unclear who, when, where, and how often APIs can be accessed. Many enterprises follow internal or external governance and compliance regulations such as the *Payment Card Industry Data Security Standard* (PCI DSS), which is a set of security standards designed to ensure that all companies that accept, process, store, or transmit credit card information maintain a secure environment. Enterprises that have to comply with such a regulation are required to document the techniques and practices used to secure the access, execution, and the management of these APIs and services in the form of rules, policies, and reports. An enterprise API platform that supports this can apply them on a companywide level and thus, contribute to be compliant to regulations.

Versioning and Revisioning

We build this great web API, expose it to the world to be used by our API users, and then realize that we made a mistake and need to introduce a breaking change in the web API. As this scenario might be rare, changes in APIs are not. Not all changes are major breaking changes and require a new version, many changes in web APIs are of a minor nature, where a new revision just needs to be tested before being officially published. The goal behind versions is to decouple API producers from API consumers. An enterprise API platform that supports versions and revisions helps API developers to let APIs evolve in a backward compatible way.

Scalability and Resiliency

When a user base grows and a company's web APIs receive more traffic than ever, there will be a point where limits are reached, and resources exhausted. While there is a number of techniques that should be considered for increasing the number of requests that can be handled such as caching and throttling, scaling the web API façade itself is one of them. When there is no other option than increasing the limits of requests that can be handled by one unit, a good enterprise API platform should be easily scalable. This is also important the other way around. Two different instances of an enterprise API platform, one in the test environment and one in production, will handle different traffic volumes. The test instance might only need to be scaled to a minimum while the production instance requires some more units.

Security

Companies that expose APIs are vulnerable to exploitation as they provide access to web services. While it is important to monitor and analyze the traffic, it is also necessary to shift the focus toward API security management and ensuring that capabilities and digital assets are protected against potential security challenges that might disrupt a business or even compromise an entire architecture. API security is a wide term and there are many strategies that a successful enterprise API platform should support such as backend authentication, excessive usage prevention, and watching abnormal activities.

DevOps

A great developer experience is an important ingredient for success. This is likewise true for API users and for API developers. As API developers, we expect short feedback loops to be able to work efficiently and for being productive which further helps us to deliver faster but also to stay motivated. As an example, as I expect a CI/CD pipeline for my RESTful web service, I expect the same automation for my web API and without the need to switch context. An enterprise API platform that supports API developers through an agile strategy for developing and operating APIs will contribute positively to the success of API products.

Performance

As an enterprise attracts more API users, the number of requests that web services must handle will probably increase as well. Depending on the capabilities, some APIs might return very individual and specific information such as user information. Those responses can be well stored on the client side if necessary and improve the performance by leveraging a client cache. Other requests may expect information that are the same for many clients such as the weather forecast for a specific location. It is advisable that those kinds of responses that are sent many times to many clients during a period of time are being cached on the server site and thus, improve the overall performance on the client's site and decrease the traffic on the server site.

Stability

An enterprise API platform decouples the APIs from the backend services. This opens for a couple of use cases in the context of API stability such as throttling and load balancing. As an example, when we understand the throughput of our traffic, we can easily throttle the throughput to a backend service by introducing rate limiting that is based on certain criteria such as an IP address from where we receive an unusually high number of requests. Another use case where a decoupled API might be useful is balancing high load between multiple backend services and thus, ensuring a stable web API. In both examples, an enterprise API platform helps to reduce the likelihood of eventual disturbances and increase the overall stability of a web API.

Introducing Azure API Management

Azure API Management is an enterprise API platform that helps to unlock digital assets and capabilities to its API consumers by routing incoming traffic to backend services no matter where they are resided, on-premises, in Azure, or at another cloud provider. Azure API Management creates an API façade for web services and serves as a front door and a single point of ingress.

Figure 2-2 shows Azure API Management as the API façade to its API consumers. The clients can be smartphone apps, desktop applications, developers, partners, or systems running on other cloud solutions. The API façade routes the incoming traffic from the clients to internal backend services such as Azure Virtual Machines, Azure

Functions Apps, Azure Kubernetes Service (AKS), but also to external services no matter if those services run on-premises or at another cloud provider. As long as Azure API Management has connectivity to the backend services, it can route the traffic. The other way around is of course also possible. Internal services running on AKS or other Azure runtime environments such as Azure Function Apps can send requests to Azure API Management if the connection allows it. We will discuss networking and how to integrate Azure API Management into different IT architectures in a later chapter.

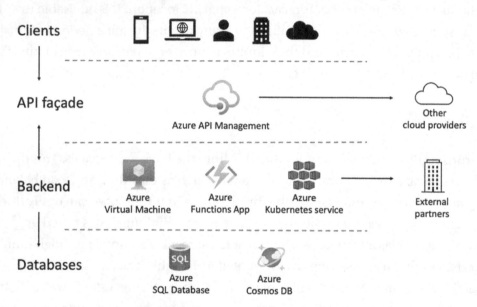

Figure 2-2. *Azure API Management as API façade*

Since all the traffic goes through Azure API Management, the scope of applications goes beyond the aspects we discussed in the previous section where we talked about the essence of enterprise API platforms. Here are some examples of what we can configure: Telemetry can be collected so requests can be traced to meter the usage, XML bodies can be transformed into JSON before being sent back to the clients, and APIs can be monetized for certain API consumers. We will discuss all these examples and more in detail throughout this book as they are important to learn for mastering this service.

Before we dive into these details, we will take a look at Azure API Management from a higher level and learn about its three main components, Azure portal, developer portal, and API gateway. It is these components that we use for configuring, administrating, managing, onboarding, security, networking, monitoring, etc., and that at the end make the traffic between API consumers and API producers flow in a predetermined and secure way.

Azure Portal

The Azure portal is an administrative web interface for provisioning and configuring Azure resources such as Azure API Management. You used the Azure portal already in the first chapter and also added your first web API. Furthermore, the Azure portal lets you manage users, APIs, and API products. We can configure the right level of API security or monitor the usage of your APIs. Most importantly, we can change the behavior of API endpoints by implementing policies. A behavior can be altering a request and response by adding a new header, setting the URL for the backend service, or validating a Json Web Token (JWT) for securely transmitting information between two parties. We will cover everything in detail throughout this book.

Interacting with Azure API Management

While the Azure portal is a great interface for getting started, checking values and doing minor changes, many companies automated their environments using Azure API Management's comprehensive REST API. Interactions with Azure API Management can be done in various ways and with many different tools and technologies such as the Azure CLI, PowerShell cmdlets, Azure Resource Manager (ARM) templates, Bicep, or the Visual Studio Code extension for Azure API Management. I will perform most of the examples in this book from the Azure Cloud Shell with PowerShell and the Azure CLI as they provide a great level of abstraction over the REST API. However, some examples will use some of the other tools and technologies depending on the use case. For example, as an API developer, the Visual Studio Code extension might be better suited for validating and testing code changes because we can do everything in the same IDE.

Before I continue and introduce the developer portal, I want to show you how to use the Azure CLI to provision a new instance of Azure API Management. Instead of using the consumption pricing tier that we have chosen the last time when we provisioned an instance directly from the Azure poral, we will this time use the developer pricing tier, as this allows us to use the developer portal.

Note   The developer pricing tier comes with a fixed cost per month. It is therefore recommended to delete the resource when it is not in use anymore. We will cover API Management pricing in a later chapter.

Figure 2-3 shows how to access the Azure Cloud Shell which is a browser-accessible shell for managing Azure resources and comes with various preinstalled tools and languages which makes it very convenient to work with from anywhere. I selected the PowerShell mode as this allows using the Azure CLI and the PowerShell cmdlets at the same time.

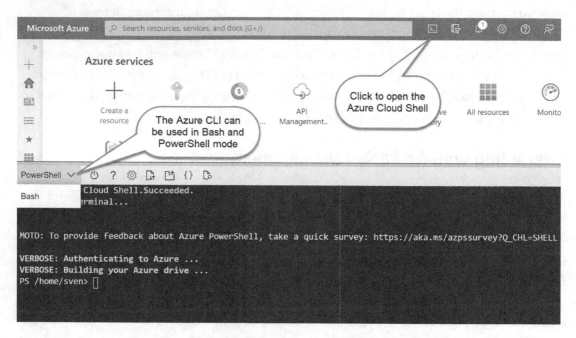

Figure 2-3. *Opening the Azure Cloud Shell in PowerShell mode*

We created already a resource group in the first chapter that we named `mastering-azure-api-management-rg`. I will reuse this resource group and deploy the new instance in this group.

Listing 2-4 shows the Azure CLI command `az apim create` for provisioning Azure API Management. The `sku-name` parameter is set to "developer" which is also the default value for the pricing tier in case you did not set it. The following parameter `no-wait` will, as the name suggests, not wait for long-running operations as it is the case in this example. Provisioning with the developer pricing tier can take up to one hour. Besides other parameters such as `publisher-name` and `publisher-email`, which both are mandatory, I also explicitly set the `subscription` parameter to ensure the right one in case you have more than one, like I have.

Listing 2-4. Provisioning Azure API Management with the Azure CLI

```
az apim create \
  --name "mastering-apim" \
  --resource-group "azure-api-management-rg" \
  --subscription "Pay-As-You-Go" \
  --no-wait \
  --sku-name "developer" \
  --publisher-name "Sven Malvik" \
  --publisher-email "sven@malvik.de" \
```

After about an hour, your instance will be up and running. We will use this instance when learning about the developer portal.

Developer Portal

One success criterion for an enterprise API platform such as Azure API Management is how it onboards its API consumers. Ideally, they sign up, select the APIs they need for solving their problems, and are then ready to go. What they typically need in the beginning when using an API for the first time is a good documentation and some examples that explain how to use an API, so they do not spend too much time figuring everything out on their own. Azure API Management supports the API consumers by providing everything an API consumer needs to know in one place and in a consistent way across all APIs.

Figure 2-4 shows the start page of the Azure API Management developer portal when visiting it the first time as an administrator. It shows that the look and feel of the developer portal can be customized, which makes it possible to style it according to a corporate brand. In this figure, I highlighted the menu so you can see one way of changing the content and style of the developer portal. Almost everything can be re-styled either in this "What You See Is What You Get" (WYSIWYG) editor or by changing the templates and stylesheets directly.

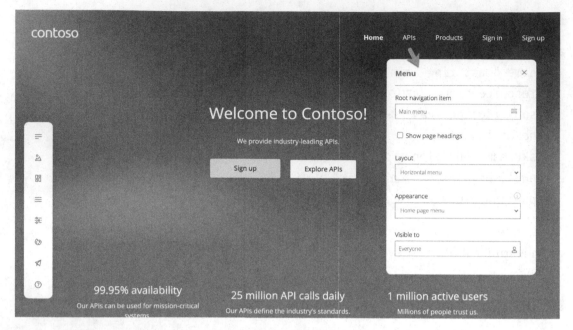

Figure 2-4. *Customizing the developer portal*

The developer portal is a website that is shipped with Azure API Management and needs to be published explicitly.

Note   The developer portal is not available in the consumption pricing tier.

Besides customizing the look and feel of the developer portal, it is also possible to add new functionality in the form of widgets. We will deep dive into the developer portal in a later chapter and learn how to administrate and customize it.

API Gateway

Azure API Management is an enterprise API platform that supports cloud-native, multi-cloud and hybrid API management. Its API gateway can be placed almost anywhere with the benefit of optimizing the API traffic flow, but also to address security and compliancy requirements. As an example, there are cases where regulations require traffic between two services to not leave the country as it could be the case where an Azure region does not exist.

Figure 2-5 shows Azure API Management and its three main components including the managed API gateway. This managed API gateway is located close to the Azure API Management instance which is not always an ideal place because of several possible reasons. Therefore, APIs can be deployed anywhere as containers making it possible to have direct communication between two services.

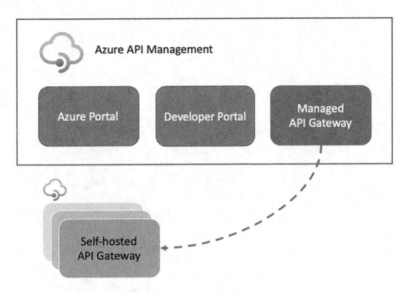

Figure 2-5. *Managed and self-hosted API gateways*

Wherever a self-hosted API gateway might be deployed, connectivity to the Azure API Management instance is still required as matrices will be uploaded and possible API changes will be applied. We will discuss how this works in detail in a later chapter.

Summary

I hope this chapter gave you a good overview of why Azure API Management can add value to your organization. This chapter started by introducing three companies and how they benefit from an enterprise API platform by making their web APIs easily consumable. You learned then the basics of web APIs, especially about SOAP and REST, as they are both supported in Azure API Management, but also because both are widely used in the industry. However, making web APIs just consumable is often not enough. Today's developers and API consumers often look at the overall experience of web APIs and want to use them right away and be productive instead of spending hours understanding them first, one by one. That's really the essence of an enterprise API platform, to create a consistent experience across many web APIs, which this chapter covered in detail. Finally, this chapter provided you with a basic introduction of Azure API Management by introducing its core components.

PART II

Key Concepts

CHAPTER 3

APIs and Products

In this chapter you will learn how to manage APIs and products so you can get started building your own API-centric organization with Azure API Management. Furthermore, you will learn how both APIs and products relate to each other as this explains how API consumers will experience your API-powered digital ecosystem from the outside.

Before we dive into each of them, APIs and products, let me briefly introduce the term "Product" in the context of Azure API Management to you. A product bundles related APIs together in the sense that an API consumer can solve a problem by using a product. As an example, a bank's payments service product may contain APIs that feature digital payments assets and capabilities such as "account balance," "money transfer," and "refund charge." A retailer may have a shop service which contains a Catalog API, an Order API, and a Cart API.

Figure 3-1 shows the relationship between products and APIs in Azure API Management. A product can be associated with many APIs as both examples demonstrated. APIs on the other side can also be associated with many products. Assume a bank that has two products, a domestic payments service and a foreign payments service. Both payments services contain the Bank API as both services need details such as the bank's name and unique identification number (BIC/SWIFT). We will discuss this in greater detail and how to set up a relation between APIs and products throughout this chapter.

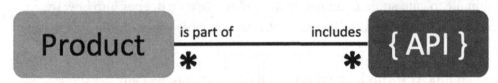

Figure 3-1. *Relation between products and APIs*

We start by discussing APIs and how to manage them from the Azure portal and from the Cloud shell with Azure CLI and Azure PowerShell before we dive into products. As the Azure CLI and Azure PowerShell for Azure API Management are based on the REST

37

© Sven Malvik 2022
S. Malvik, *Mastering Azure API Management*, https://doi.org/10.1007/978-1-4842-8011-9_3

API of Azure API Management, it may happen that those abstractions fall behind and are missing features such as tagging APIs. In those cases, we will use the REST API directly.

Other ways of managing APIs are by defining Bicep or ARM templates. ARM templates are often challenging for the web service developers who create the backend APIs. Ideally, it is those developers that deploy their own APIs to Azure API Management. Using ARM templates, they would need to write those ARM templates which is often not their main technical domain and therefore harder to implement. However, we will cover deploying APIs with ARM templates when discussing policies in a later chapter.

In comparison, Bicep templates are easier to implement and maintain by most developers as they abstract away many of the more cumbersome concepts of ARM templates. Bicep is also where Microsoft puts its effort and has become quite popular among cloud engineers who define Azure infrastructure as code.

You remember from the previous chapters that we already provisioned two instances of Azure API Management, one with the consumption pricing tier and the other with the developer pricing tier. Both are identical when it comes to managing APIs and products. The same is true for all the other pricing tiers. However, the following chapters build upon the APIs and products we will create in this chapter where the consumption pricing tier is not always sufficient. The developer portal is one example that we will discuss in a later chapter where we can't use the consumption pricing tier. For that reason, I will use the developer pricing tier in this chapter. In case you would like to go with the consumption pricing tier, remember that you will need to recreate some products and APIs in a later chapter.

APIs

In the first chapter, you already created the Conference API by importing an OpenAPI definition file to gain some first experience. Before we dive deeper into how we can create and configure APIs, let me briefly explain what other options of creating APIs exist:

- **Blank API**: This is an empty API that does not reflect any backend API. It can be useful for scenarios where a backend API is not in place yet and need to be mocked.

- **OpenAPI**: This is for modern RESTful backend APIs that are defined by this specification either in YAML or JSON format.

- **WADL**: An XML representation of a contract between a client and a server.

- **WSDL**: This is an XML description format for SOAP-based web services used primarily by older APIs.

- **Logic App**: An Azure resource type for defining interactions and workflows.

- **App Service**: This is a web-hosted service for building RESTful web services.

- **Function App**: Azure's serverless solution for building various types of applications such as web APIs.

In the following sections, we will learn to manage APIs. We start by creating a blank API with the Azure CLI and discuss all details. From there, we will learn how to manage APIs with PowerShell. Finally, we will see how to create APIs from backend Azure resources such as Logic App, App Service, and Function App.

Create Blank API with Azure CLI

In this section, we will use the Azure CLI from the Azure Cloud Shell to create a blank API and then add operations to it that map endpoints to a backend API. As we don't have a backend API yet, we will use this API later when we talk about policies to mock a backend web service.

We start by repeating the steps from the first chapter where we logged into the Azure Cloud Shell. Alternatively, you can *install the Azure CLI on your local machine* by following the steps in the Azure documentation. As we are using the Azure CLI for now, you can either select the "Bash" or "PowerShell" mode, both will work in the same way.

Listing 3-1 shows how to ensure that you are using the current subscription that contains the provisioned Azure API Management instance that you want to use. If you just created an account, you won't have more than the "Pay-As-You-Go" subscription, so you might skip this step. Otherwise, you will need to set the correct subscription. Verify at the end that your Azure API Management instance does exist by running the `az apim list` command.

Listing 3-1. Verify and set the correct subscription

```
# Verify the current subscription
az account show

# Set the correct subscription
az account set –subscription <YOUR_SUBSCRIPTION_ID>

# List the name of all instances in the current subscription
az apim list --query [].name
```

Now that you are in the correct subscription and have verified that your Azure API Management instance exists, you are able to create a new API by using the `az apim api create` command.

Listing 3-2 uses this command with some main parameters for creating an API. We will discuss the remaining optional parameters in later chapters, where we will learn about different aspects such as subscriptions and security.

- The `service-name` parameter is the name of the Azure API Management instance. You retrieved it from the previous command where you listed all instances.

- The `resource-group` is the container that holds your instance.

- You can set the `api-id` by yourself. It is a unique API identifier across an Azure API Management instance.

- The `display-name` is what the API consumer will see in the developer portal for an API.

- The `description` tells the API consumers what this API is about and makes it an important part of an API. As this will be displayed in the developer portal, it supports HTML tags.

- The `path` parameter is the context-path that follows a URI.

- You used the master subscription key in the first chapter. Now, we set the `subscription-key-required` parameter to false so we can access it directly.

Listing 3-2. Create API with Azure CLI

```
az apim api create `
     --service-name mastering-apim `
     --resource-group mastering-apim-rg `
     --api-id my-demo-api `
     --display-name "My Demo API" `
     --description "This is an <b>API for testing</b>" `
     --path "demo" `
     --subscription-key-required false
```

As a result, you will get a JSON object with all settings that confirms a successful operation. This newly created API does, of course, nothing yet as we have not added any operation to it that we could use for mocking a backend API endpoint. We will change that now and add a simple GET operation with the `az apim api operation create` command.

Add API Operation

Listing 3-3 uses this command with the parameters necessary for creating an operation that we will then use for mocking a backend API endpoint. We have already discussed some parameters in the previous example where we created an API. The following parameters are special for creating an operation:

- The `api-id` that the operation will be added to.

- You can set the `operation-id` by yourself. It is a unique identifier across an Azure API Management instance.

- The `display-name` is what the API consumer will see in the developer portal for this operation.

- The `description` tells the API consumers what this operation is about and makes it an important part of an operation. As this will be displayed in the developer portal, it supports HTML tags.

- The `url-template` parameter is part of the URL and can contain parameters in curly braces.

- In case you set parameters in the "url-template" parameter, you must set the `params` parameter and with the same name and the type.

Listing 3-3. Create an operation with Azure CLI

```
az apim api operation create `
    --method GET `
    --service-name mastering-apim `
    --resource-group mastering-apim-rg `
    --api-id my-demo-api `
    --operation-id my-demo-operation `
    --display-name "My Demo Operation" `
    --description "This is a <b>Operation for testing</b>" `
    --url-template "/demo-operation/{pname}/{pvalue}" `
    --params name=pname description="Test1" type=paramType `
    --params name=pvalue description="Test 2" type=string
```

Even though we were able to add an operation to the API, we won't be able to use it yet as it does not process requests in any way. We will change this by adding a mock response for this operation and by defining a simple policy. Policies will be discussed in detail in a separate chapter, so we won't go into the details here.

Figure 3-2 shows an easy way of adding a mock response for an API operation by selecting the newly added operation "My Demo Operation" and clicking "+ Add policy" in the "Inbound processing" section within the Azure portal.

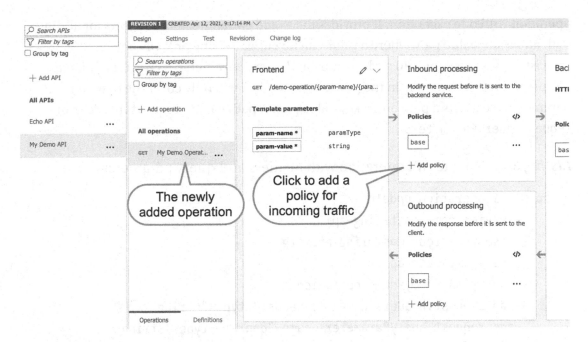

Figure 3-2. *Adding a policy to an API operation*

You will now be presented a list of options for changing the behavior of incoming traffic through policies for this API operation only. Select the option mock-response and confirm the setting "API Management response" with the value "200 OK, application/json" by clicking the "Save" button. All incoming traffic for this API operation will now return an HTTP status code 200. As mentioned previously, we will discuss policies in great detail in a later chapter. Try to access the API operation now by sending the following request, remember to change the service-name "mastering-apim" to yours:

```
curl -i https://mastering-apim.azure-api.net/demo/demo-operation/testkey/
testvalue
```

If you have done everything right, you will retrieve a HTTP/1.1 200 OK response back, which means you have done everything right.

Update API Operation

You may have noticed in the previous example that we have not included headers or query parameters. We will do this in the next example, where we will update the API operation that we already created by using the az apim api operation update command. This command works exactly the same way as if we would create an API operation with one exception. It provides the `--add` parameter which allows for adding a path and a key-value pair, where a value can be either a string or JSON object.

Listing 3-4 shows how to add a header and query parameter. As we already have discussed most parameters in the previous example, I will only cover the new `add` parameter. It expects a path and a key-value pair. A path can be `request.headers` or `request.queryParameters`.

Listing 3-4. Update API operation with headers and query parameters

```
az apim api operation update `
    --service-name mastering-apim `
    --resource-group mastering-apim-rg `
    --api-id my-demo-api `
    --operation-id my-demo-operation `
    --add request.headers name="my-header" type="string" `
    --add request.queryParameters name="qparam" type="string"
```

Updating an API operation lets you add and change properties as we have seen but also change the other settings such as `description`, `display-name`, `method`, and the `url-template`.

Manage APIs with Azure PowerShell

Now that you have gained some experience with the `az apim api` command, I want to briefly introduce you to the Azure PowerShell module. Azure PowerShell is already preinstalled in the Azure Cloud Shell, so you can start immediately using it. In case you prefer to work from your local machine, follow the instructions to *install the Azure Az PowerShell module.*

When performing a change on an instance of Azure API Management with Azure PowerShell, you will need to provide a context. A context is saying where and on what instance you want to perform a change. You might have already set the correct subscription with the `az` command in the previous examples; however, the Azure PowerShell module has its own context. If you have only one subscription because you just created a new Azure account, you might skip this step. Otherwise, you need to get the right subscription first and then loading into a variable:

```
$context = Get-AzSubscription -SubscriptionId <SUBSCRIPTION_ID>
```

You can then set the context as follows:

```
Set-AzContext $context
```

Finally, you will use the `New-AzApiManagementContext` cmdlet to set the context for working on the correct instance.

Listing 3-5 shows the complete example of setting the context for an instance of Azure API Management. After executing both cmdlets, `Get-AzSubscription` and `Set-AzContext`, you set the context for your Azure API Management instance by loading it into a variable. You will need this context variable whenever you run a cmdlet on your Azure API Management instance. As you already have set the correct subscription, you need to set the resource group (`-ResourceGroupName`) and the service name (`-ServiceName`) as parameters. Remember to change both variables to your values.

Listing 3-5. Setting the context of your Azure API Management instance

```
# Get subscription
$context = Get-AzSubscription -SubscriptionId <SUBSCRIPTION_ID>

# Set subscription by setting the context
Set-AzContext $context

# Set context for Azure API Management instance
$apimContext = New-AzApiManagementContext `
    -ResourceGroupName mastering-apim-rg `
    -ServiceName mastering-apim
```

It is now time to perform changes on this context. You might remember the Demo Conference API that we imported in the first chapter. The PowerShell cmdlet for this operation is `Import-AzApiManagementApi`. The parameters are the same as you have set in the Azure portal.

- The `Context` which tells what Azure API Management instance to perform changes on.

- The `ApiId` is a unique identifier across this instance. If not set, Azure API Management will assign a random string.

- The specification format (`SpecificationFormat`) accepts "Swagger,"
  "WADL," "WSDL," "OpenApi," and "OpenApiJson." As the Conference
  Demo API is in JSON format, I set it to "OpenApiJson."

- The `Path` is the context path of the URL. In this example, I set it
  to "conf," which results in this URL: `https://conferenceapi.`
  `azurewebsites.net/conf`

```
Import-AzApiManagementApi `
    -Context $apimContext `
    -ApiId conf-api `
    -SpecificationFormat "OpenApiJson" `
    -SpecificationUrl "https://conferenceapi.azurewebsites.net/?format=json" `
    -Path "conf"
```

Running this API import cmdlet will add the Demo Conference API to your instance
the same way as you did from the Azure portal. Even though it is a convenient way to
perform changes from the Azure portal, PowerShell enables to automate repetitive tasks
such as import and delete. We will cover this topic in detail in a later topic.

Let us now clean up and delete this API by executing the following Remove-
AzApiManagementApi cmdlet. It requires two parameters, the context (`Context`) and the
API identifier (`ApiId`):

```
Remove-AzApiManagementApi `
    -Context $apimContext `
    -ApiId conf-api
```

The Azure PowerShell module provides many more cmdlets. Many of them will be
covered throughout this book in detailed chapters. For now, we have covered the basics
of managing APIs with PowerShell.

Create API from Azure Resources

You have learned how to define an API from the Azure portal and how to create an API
from a definition file such as OpenAPI. Another way of creating an API is by creating
a link to an existing Azure resource that exposes a web API. Azure API Management
provides three resource types for that purpose that can be linked directly from the Azure

portal, Logic App, Function App, and App Service. The way you create an API from an existing Azure resource is the same for all three resource types.

In the following section, you will learn how to create an API from an Azure App Service web application. Furthermore, you will learn why there are additional configurations necessary to ensure that incoming traffic to your web application is coming from your Azure API Management instance and from anywhere else.

Create Web Application in Azure App Service

Before you create an API from an Azure resource in the Azure portal, let us create a basic Azure App Service web application in three simple steps by using the Azure CLI again from the Azure Cloud shell. An Azure App Service plan defines a set of compute resources for a web application to run. You will use the free pricing tier as you will use it only for the purpose of this example.

Listing 3-6 shows the complete example of creating an Azure App Service web application. You will first create a resource group by using the `az group create` command with the location and name as parameters. Secondly, you will need an App Service plan which can be created with `az appservice plan create`. The command requires a name, the resource group, and the pricing tier, SKU, which you can set to "FREE." Finally, you will create the web application itself by executing the `az webapp create` command. Additional to the name and resource group, it requires the App Service plan. In this example, I called the App Service plan "mywebappplan" and the web application "mywebapp."

Listing 3-6. Creating an Azure App Service web application

```
# Create a resource group
az group create --location westeurope --name mywebapp-rg

# Create an App Service plan in FREE tier
az appservice plan create --name mywebappplan --resource-group
mywebapp-rg --sku FREE

# Create a web app
az webapp create --name mywebapp0815 --resource-group mywebapp-rg --plan
mywebappplan
```

The web application that is created by default comes with a static website and a web API. You can now test your web application in a browser by using the URL `<WEBAPP_NAME>.azurewebsites.net`, as shown in Figure 3-3.

Figure 3-3. *Publicly accessible web application*

If you created successfully a web application with Azure App Service, congratulations. Otherwise, you can *create a web app* by follow the steps in the official documentation.

Create API from Azure App Service Web Application

Now that you have an App Service web application in place, let us create an API directly from the Azure portal. Repeat the steps from the first chapter where you imported an API from an OpenAPI definition file. This time, you will select the "App Service" option instead of the "OpenAPI" option.

The last time when you imported the OpenAPI file, you set the URL of the Demo Conference API definition file. This time, you will click the browse button and select an Azure resource, your web application. The display-name and name will be automatically set. As API URL suffix, set the context-path for this API as you have done with the Demo Conference API.

Figure 3-4 shows a successfully created API for the Azure App Service web application. The default web application comes already with some API operations. Click on "All operations" to see the policy for it. As mentioned earlier, policies will be discussed in detail in a later chapter. I just wanted to show how the API and the web application are linked with each other.

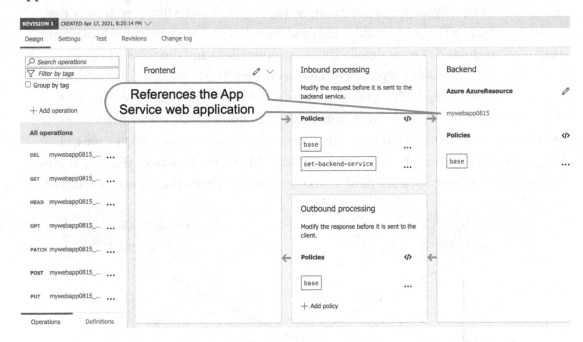

Figure 3-4. *An API policy is linking to an Azure resource*

Another way of creating an API from an Azure resource is by defining a Bicep or ARM template. We will discuss the topic of deploying APIs with Bicep and ARM templates in a later chapter, where you will learn about API development in the context of Azure API Management.

Products

In the beginning of this chapter, we discussed briefly the term "product" in the context of Azure API Management. In this section, we will discuss them in greater detail and learn how to manage them and how to add related APIs to a product that API consumers then can subscribe to.

Note   A product bundles a set of APIs that API consumers can gain access to through subscriptions.

Before we dive into technical discussions, let us briefly repeat how APIs and products relate to each other by looking at an example. Figure 3-5 shows a fictive web store that has three APIs. The Cart API contains the product items a user has selected and wants to buy, the Products API gives details about a product item and the Sales API gives information about how many products have been sold. The users of the fictive store may only access the Cart API and the Products API through the web store. The store administrators of the web store may only access the Products API and the Sales API. To make this work in Azure API Management, we create two products, one that we call "Shopping Service," and which includes the Cart API and the Products API, and another that we call "Administration Service," which contains the Products API and the Sales API.

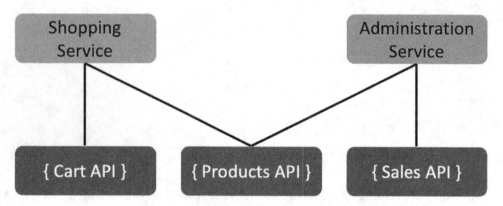

Figure 3-5. *Example of a products to APIs relation*

API consumers such as the website of the web store and the administrators of the web store will subscribe to either the Shopping Service or the Administrator Service. We will use the following three subsections to demonstrate how to implement the example of Figure 3-5.

Create APIs

Before we look into how to create products and add APIs, we need to create those APIs. You can do this in the same way as you did with the "My Demo API," where you used the `az apim api create` command with the Azure CLI. Run this command three times for each API. Alternatively, you can use Azure PowerShell, as the example in Listing 3-7 shows. Before you can run the example from the Azure Cloud Shell, execute the code from Listing 3-5 for setting the context for Azure API Management.

Listing 3-7 shows how to use Azure PowerShell for creating the three APIs in a Foreach loop with the `New-AzApiManagementApi` cmdlet. The cmdlet for creating an API uses the following parameters:

- The `Context` parameter informs the cmdlet what Azure API Management instance to use. Follow the code example of Listing 3-5 for how to set the context.

- `ApiId` is a unique API identifier across an Azure API Management instance.

- The `Name` and the `Description` is what an API consumer will be displayed in the developer portal.

- The `Path` parameter is the context path of the URL.

- The `ServiceUrl` tells where a request to route to. It is the URL of the backend web service. As this is just an example for learning about products, you can set this to a random URL for now.

- As protocols, you can set http or https.

Listing 3-7. Creating three APIs with Azure PowerShell

```
$apis = "cart", "products", "sales"
Foreach ($currentApi in $apis) {
    New-AzApiManagementApi `
        -Context $apimContext `
        -ApiId $currentApi-api `
        -Name $currentApi `
        -Description "$currentApi <b>API for testing</b>" `
        -Path "$currentApi" `
        -ServiceUrl "http://$currentApi.xyz/backend" `
        -Protocols @("http", "https")
}
```

You should see three new APIs, "cart-api," "products-api," and "sales-api." Verify this by running the `Get-AzApiManagementApi` cmdlet and then pipe the output for filtering the ApiId, as the following code shows:

```
Get-AzApiManagementApi -Context $apimContext | Select-Object ApiId
```

Now that you have all three APIs, we can continue and create the products so we can add the APIs to them.

Create Products

The next step in implementing Figure 3-5 is to create two products, "Shopping Service" and "Administrator Service." You can do this in almost the same way as you did when you created the APIs. This time, you will use the PowerShell cmdlet `New-AzApiManagementProduct` surrounded by a Foreach loop for both products.

Listing 3-8 shows how to use the Foreach loop for creating two products in Azure API Management with Azure PowerShell. The example reuses the `Context` parameter from Listing 3-5. This cmdlet requires the `Title` and `Description` parameters for displaying in the developer portal. It also sets the unique identifier for the product, `ProductId`. The last parameter, `State`, indicates whether the product is discoverable in the developer portal or just visible for an administrator.

Listing 3-8. Creating two products with Azure PowerShell

```
$products = "shopping", "administrator"
Foreach ($currentProduct in $products) {
    New-AzApiManagementProduct -Context $apimContext `
        -Title "$currentProduct service" `
        -Description "This is the $currentProduct service" `
        -ProductId $currentProduct-service `
        -State published
}
```

You might want to verify if both products were created by executing the following code:

```
Get-AzApiManagementProduct -Context $apimContext | Select-Object ProductId
```

You might have expected two new products. Instead, the response listed two additional products: "Starter" and "Unlimited." Both products are built in and shall help to get started. Both products also have subscriptions that are associated. As we have not yet discussed subscriptions, you can delete them as well by running the Remove-AzApiManagementProduct cmdlet with the parameters "ProductId" and "DeleteSubscriptions," as shown in the following:

```
# Deletes the product: Unlimited
Remove-AzApiManagementProduct -Context $apimContext `
    -ProductId Unlimited `
    -DeleteSubscriptions

# Deletes the product: Starter
Remove-AzApiManagementProduct -Context $apimContext `
    -ProductId Starter `
    -DeleteSubscriptions
```

Executing the Get-AzApiManagementProduct cmdlet again should now result in only the two products that you created by yourself.

Add APIs to Products

As products bundle APIs, the final step for implementing Figure 3-5 is to add the right APIs to the right products. We do this by using the Add-AzApiManagementApiToProduct cmdlet of Azure PowerShell. The cmdlet requires three parameters: "Context," "ApiId," and "ProductId."

- You set the Context of the current Azure API Management instance by following the example of Listing 3-5.

- The ApiId of the API to be added to the product.

- The ProductId of the product that you want to add the API to.

Listing 3-9 shows an example of implementing the relations between APIs and products, as shown in Figure 3-5. The example defines two Foreach loops, one for each product, and iterates through $apis which in case of the Shopping Service are the Cart API and Products API. It then calls the mentioned cmdlet for adding the current API to the product.

Listing 3-9. Example of adding APIs to products

```
# Add APIs to Shopping Service
$product = "shopping-service"
$apis = "cart-api", "products-api"

Foreach ($currentApi in $apis) { `
    Add-AzApiManagementApiToProduct -Context $apimContext `
        -ApiId $currentApi `
        -ProductId $product
}

# Add APIs to Administrator Service
$product = "administrator-service"
$apis = "products-api", "sales-api"

Foreach ($currentApi in $apis) { `
    Add-AzApiManagementApiToProduct -Context $apimContext `
        -ApiId $currentApi `
        -ProductId $product
}
```

Summary

Congratulations, you have learned how to manage APIs and products in the context of Azure API Management. You have also learned how to create a relation between them so API consumers can access only the APIs that are added to the products they have subscribed to. Even though you have not learned about the concept of subscriptions yet, you have already seen parts of it. Some Azure PowerShell cmdlets such as `Remove-AzApiManagementProduct` require subscription-related information such as `DeleteSubscriptions`. You will learn about subscriptions in a later chapter when you learn how to manage users and groups.

CHAPTER 4

Users and Groups

We have talked about APIs and products and how to manage them in the previous chapter. In this chapter, you will learn how to manage the consumers of the APIs, the users. You will learn to group the users so you can simplify the access to APIs and how the users and groups relate to the products and APIs. As you have already learned the relation between APIs and products in the previous chapter, we will skip this discussion.

Users relate to groups like APIs to products. As products bundle related APIs together in the sense that an API consumer can solve a problem by using a product, groups bundle related users together in the sense that the users of a group can access the same APIs within products.

As an example, users that belong to the same partner organization could reside in one group. As you have many partner organizations that want to use your APIs, you will have many groups. Products that can be accessed by certain groups will then be associated with these groups.

Figure 1-4 shows the relation between users, groups, products, and APIs in more detail. A user can be part of many groups that can be associated to many products. Users that are within a group can see only those products in the developer portal and subscribe to them that have associated accessible groups to them. You will learn everything about subscriptions and the developer portal in separate chapters.

© Sven Malvik 2022
S. Malvik, *Mastering Azure API Management*, https://doi.org/10.1007/978-1-4842-8011-9_4

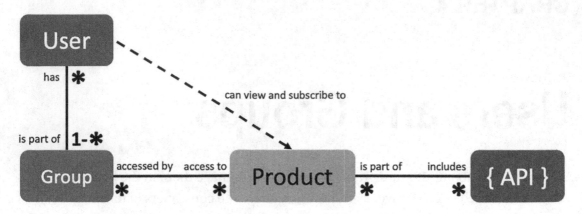

Figure 4-1. *Relation between groups, users, products, and APIs*

As you now understand the relation between users, groups, products, and APIs, we will use the following two sections to learn how to manage users and groups and how to associate them to products. You will use Azure PowerShell from within the Azure Cloud Shell.

Note   Users and groups are not part of the Consumption pricing tier.

Follow the steps in Listing 3-5 to set the context of your Azure API Management instance that you want to use. Remember that you will need an Azure API Management instance with one of the other pricing tiers and not the consumption pricing tier. In Listing 2-4, you learned how to provision Azure API Management with the developer pricing tier by using the Azure CLI.

Groups

In Azure API Management, groups are used to manage the visibility of products in the developer portal. Users who are in a group that is associated to a certain product can see and subscribe to this product. There exist already three immutable system groups, administrators, developers, and guests. You can also create custom groups such as groups for partner organizations or groups for your internal developers who need access to an internal Azure API Management product. Furthermore, groups can also be created from an external identity provider like Azure Active Directory.

System Groups

System groups are immutable. They can neither be changed nor deleted, and users get added and removed automatically by the system. Listing 4-1 shows how to list all groups by running the Azure PowerShell cmdlet `Get-AzApiManagementGroup`.

Listing 4-1. List all groups

```
Get-AzApiManagementGroup -Context $apimContext | Select-Object GroupId,Type
```

As we have not created a custom group yet, the result of `Get-AzApiManagementGroup` lists three groups, administrators, developers, and guests. These groups are of type "System."

- **Administrators** include the Azure subscription owners.

- **Developers** include all users that have signed up in the developer portal or have been invited.

- **Guests** include unauthenticated users. Products that are associated to this group should either not require a subscription or the products associated to it will serve as documentation only.

Create a Group

A group can be created by using the Azure PowerShell cmdlet `New-AzApiManagementGroup`. As mentioned at the beginning of this section ("Groups"), there are three different types of groups, system, custom, and external. A custom group is a type of group that has no dependencies to other Azure resources or systems and can be created by setting the parameter "type" to "Custom."

Listing 4-2 shows how to create a custom group. The cmdlet uses the following parameters:

- The `Context` which tells what Azure API Management instance to perform changes on.

- The `GroupId` is a unique identifier across this instance. If not set, Azure API Management will assign a random string.

57

- The Name and the description are what a user will be displayed in the developer portal.

- The Type can either be "Custom" or "External."

Listing 4-2. Create a custom group

```
New-AzApiManagementGroup `
    -Context $apimContext `
    -GroupId internal `
    -Name Internal `
    -Description "Internal developers" `
    -Type Custom
```

You can see your new custom group in the Azure portal or by running the code of Listing 4-1. It lists all group identifiers and their types. If you have followed this book, you should see three system groups and one custom group.

External groups can be created by setting the parameter "Type" to "External" and the parameter "ExternalId" to the identifier of the group from the external identity provider. An external identity provider can be added with the Azure PowerShell cmdlet New-AzApiManagementIdentityProvider. As of writing of this book, Azure Active Directory is the only external provider that should be used. Other external identity providers such as Facebook, Twitter, Google, and Microsoft are deprecated and might disappear in the near future. We will not use Azure Active Directory as an identity provider and will use system and custom groups throughout this book.

Associate Groups to Products

Even though we have created groups and products, the users within the groups can't see any of the products in the developer portal yet, so they can't use them yet. We can change that by associating groups to products. A group that has access to a product can be seen by the users in the developer portal, so they can subscribe to the product. You will learn about the developer portal and subscriptions in a later chapter.

The Azure PowerShell cmdlet Add-AzApiManagementProductToGroup adds a group to a product by using the "groupId" and the "productId" parameters. Listing 4-3 shows an example of adding the product "shopping-service" to the system group "guests" in the Azure API Management instance that is provided by the "Context" parameter from Listing 3-5.

Listing 4-3. Associating a group to a product

```
Add-AzApiManagementProductToGroup `
    -Context $apimContext `
    -GroupId guests `
    -ProductId shopping-service
```

Only unauthenticated users will be able to see the shopping-service with its APIs in the developer portal. In case an API within this product requires a subscription for using, a user must sign in first. As authenticated users are not guests anymore, users will not see this product anymore which means that at least a second group, "Developers," needs to be added.

Try also to add your new internal group to the product "Administrator Service" by running the same code from Listing 4-3 with a different `GroupId` and `ProductId` parameter.

```
Add-AzApiManagementProductToGroup `
    -Context $apimContext `
    -GroupId internal `
    -ProductId administrator-service
```

We will use this association in the next section where we will discuss users.

Users

Users are the consumers of the APIs. Some APIs might not require a subscription and can be accessed directly by authenticated and unauthenticated users. In this section, you will learn how to create users with Azure PowerShell. Furthermore, you will learn to deactivate and reactivate a user account. Lastly, you will add a user to a group, so products can be made visible to them in the developer portal. The developer portal is also the place where users normally would sign up or reset their password. You will learn about the developer portal in a later chapter.

Before we start and create a new user, let us see what users already exist by using the Azure PowerShell cmdlet `Get-AzApiManagementUser`. As you will list all users, the only parameter that is necessary is the context parameter.

Listing 4-4 pipes the result to the `Select-Object` cmdlet to print out the first name, email, user identifier, and the state of the user.

Listing 4-4. Listing all users

```
Get-AzApiManagementUser -Context $apimContext | Select-Object FirstName,Email,
UserId,State
```

If you have not yet created any user either from the Azure portal or programmatically, the result lists only one user, the Administrator, with the email address and the UserId of 1. The administrator is by default an active user who is already in the "Administrator" group.

Create a User

You will now create a new user with Azure PowerShell. As previously mentioned, the self-service of the developer portal lets API users create users by themselves where they fill out a form and then confirm an email they will receive to the address they provided in the form. This is different with Azure PowerShell. By using the latest version of Azure PowerShell, a user won't receive an email. However, this can be achieved by using the Azure REST API for Azure API Management.

Listing 4-5 shows how to create a user with the Azure PowerShell cmdlet `New-AzApiManagementUser`. Besides the parameters such as a unique "UserId" which is optional, "FirstName," "LastName," "Email," and the "Context" (see Listing 3-5), this cmdlet requires a secure password. A password can be secured by reading text from the console with the cmdlet `Read-Host` and setting the parameter `AsSecureString`.

Listing 4-5. Creating a user

```
$securePassword = Read-Host -AsSecureString

New-AzApiManagementUser `
      -Context $apimContext `
      -UserId jon-falk-0815 `
      -FirstName Jon `
      -LastName Falk `
      -Email mastering-apim@malvik.de `
      -Password $securePassword
```

After you have successfully executed the code of Listing 4-5, run the `Get-AzApiManagementUser` of Listing 4-4 once again. Even though we have not set the state of this new user, it is active by default. This is different to the developer portal where a new user will first be in state "Pending" until a confirmation mail was confirmed.

Deactivate and Reactivate a User

Let us now assume that this user has not paid the bill for the last month and you want to block the user for now. This can be achieved by changing the state of this user from **Active** to **Blocked** by using the Azure PowerShell cmdlet `Set-AzApiManagementUser`.

```
Set-AzApiManagementUser `
    -Context $apimContext `
    -UserId jon-falk-0815 `
    -State Blocked
```

After executing this cmdlet, the user will neither be able to access the developer portal nor call any API. Once the user has started paying bills again, you would execute the same code with the state **Active**. The user can now use the developer portal again and call the APIs the user has access to.

Add a User to a Group

You learned previously that products are made visible to groups in the developer portal. It is therefore necessary to add a user to one or several groups, so that a user is able to subscribe to a product. We will discuss subscriptions and the developer portal in later chapters.

The following code shows how to add a user to a group by using the `Add-AzApiManagementUserToGroup` cmdlet of Azure PowerShell. Run the code from Listing 3-5 first for setting the context of the Azure API Management instance you will use. The cmdlet requires, in addition to the context, also the `GroupId` and the `UserId` parameters as shown in the following:

```
Add-AzApiManagementUserToGroup `
    -Context $apimContext `
    -GroupId internal `
    -UserId jon-falk-0815
```

The user "Jon Falk" is now in the internal group that is associated to the product "Administrator Service." Jon Falk can now see the product and its APIs in the developer portal and is able to subscribe to it, which we will discuss in detail in later chapters.

Summary

In this chapter, you learned not only how to manage users and groups with Azure PowerShell but also how they relate to products and APIs in Azure API Management.

CHAPTER 5

Versions and Revisions

As we change and improve our backend applications over time, add new features and remove some others, we might come to a point where we have to make changes to the backend APIs as well. Some of them might be breaking changes and require an API consumer to change code on the client side, while other changes are non-breaking changes where API consumers can decide whether they want to change the client side and eventually use a new feature or not.

Azure API Management supports both breaking and non-breaking changes by using the concepts of versions and revisions. Versions can be used for breaking changes while revisions can be used for non-breaking changes.

In this chapter, we will learn the concepts of both in the context of Azure API Management and how to create and use them. Before we delve into each of them, let us look at how they relate to each other.

Figure 5-1 shows three entities, **Versions Set**, **Version**, and **Revision**. A version set is a representation of a set of versions for a single API, in this example, API v1 and API v2. A version set defines how a version can be requested. A version on the other side is its own API with its own API identifier. Each version has at least one revision, the current revision with the identifier of 1 that is shown as r1 in this example. Other revisions can be requested by appending `;rev=<ID>` at the end of the URL.

© Sven Malvik 2022
S. Malvik, *Mastering Azure API Management*, https://doi.org/10.1007/978-1-4842-8011-9_5

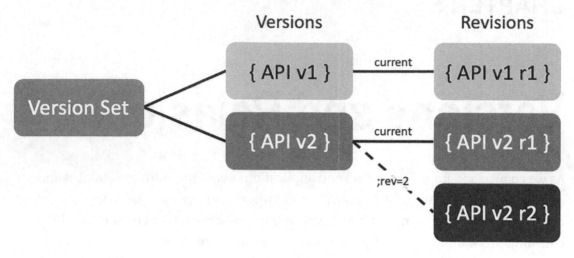

Figure 5-1. *Relation between API versions and API revisions*

In the following sections, we will delve into both of them, versions and revisions, and learn how to create them with Azure PowerShell and how to request them individually.

Versions

Versions can be used for communicating breaking changes to the API consumers. An example of a breaking change could be as simple as changing an endpoints URI from /getcustomer/<ID> to /customer/<ID>. Clients that still call the *old* URI would receive the HTTP status code 404, resource not found. There are at least two options of attacking a breaking change:

1. Leverage the power of policies in Azure API Management and rewrite a request to the new URI of the backend API.

2. Introduce a new version in Azure API Management with the changed URI and communicate it to the API consumers.

The first option is saying that an API consumer won't notice any change because the API façade did not change. Instead, Azure API Management would rewrite the request and call the backend API with the new URI. This approach increases the complexity because a policy needs to be implemented that makes this rewrite happen. We will discuss Azure API Management policies in detail in a later chapter and focus in this chapter on API versions, option 2.

In option 2, an API consumer would choose between different API versions where each version is a new API that has its own unique identifier.

Version Scheme

Before we create a new version of an API, let us discuss how to call a new version. Azure API Management offers three different version schemes for that matter:

1. **Path-based** where the version is part of the URL

2. **Header-based** where the version is set as a header

3. **Query-based** where the version is set as a query parameter in the URL

Listing 5-1 shows how to define a version scheme by creating a **Version Set** with the Azure PowerShell cmdlet New-AzApiManagementApiVersionSet. A version set represents a set of API versions for a single logical API like the Demo Conference API. Besides the parameters such as the context of Azure API Management and a name, Listing 5-1 sets the mandatory version scheme Scheme and an optional identifier ApiVersionSetId. I set the version scheme to **Segment**, which means that I went for the path-based scheme. The other options would be **Header** for header-based scheme and **Query** for query-based scheme.

Listing 5-1. Creating a version set

```
New-AzApiManagementApiVersionSet `
    -Context $apimContext `
    -Name "Demo Conference API" `
    -Scheme Segment `
    -ApiVersionSetId conf-api-vs
```

An API that we want to be represented by this version set requires the ApiVersionSetId. Let us see how to do this when adding the Demo Conference API as a version.

Add a New Version

A prerequisite for creating an API version is a version set, as Listing 5-1 showed. As mentioned at the beginning of this section ("Versions"), a version is a unique API with its own unique identifier. You can therefore create a version in the same way as you did when you created an API, by using the Azure PowerShell cmdlet `Import-AzApiManagementApi`. The difference now is that you must add the `ApiVersionSetId` parameters from Listing 5-1 and a version number, `ApiVersion` that you choose yourself.

Note   When adding a new API version in the Azure portal, a version set is added automatically.

Before you create a new version, let us re-import the Demo Conference API from Chapter 3 and add this API to your version set, as the following example demonstrates:

```
Import-AzApiManagementApi `
    -Context $apimContext `
    -ApiId conf-api `
    -SpecificationFormat "OpenApiJson" `
    -SpecificationUrl "https://conferenceapi.azurewebsites.
    net/?format=json" `
    -Path "conf" `
    -ApiVersionSetId conf-api-vs
```

The way you would call this API has not changed in any way as it is still your original API. Let us now add a new version v1 by creating a copy of this API with the Azure PowerShell cmdlet `New-AzApiManagementApi`. There are two parameters that are interesting: `SourceApiId` which is the API identifier of the API that you want to copy from, and `ApiVersion` that I set to v1. Notice that the parameter `Path` is still the same, `conf`.

```
New-AzApiManagementApi `
    -Context $apimContext `
    -ApiId conf-api-v1 `
    -Name "Demo Conference API" `
    -ServiceUrl http://YOUR_NEW_BACKEND_API `
    -Path conf `
```

```
    -Protocols @("http", "https") `
    -ApiVersionSetId conf-api-vs `
    -SourceApiId conf-api `
    -ApiVersion v1
```

The URL of this new path-based version (/v1) has changed to *http(s):*
// mastering-apim.azure-api.net/conf/v1/topics.

Note   Calling this endpoint will respond with an HTTP status code 401 as it requires a subscription key. We will discuss subscriptions in the following chapter.

As every new version has its own unique API identifier (ApiId), it can be added to products in the same way as un-versioned APIs by using the Azure PowerShell cmdlet AzApiManagementApiToProduct, as Listing 3-9 shows.

Revisions

Revisions are a way of communicating non-breaking changes to API consumers. Adding an endpoint to an existing version would, for example, not require a client side to change its code because no existing endpoint has changed. As Figure 5-1 shows, every API and every version has at least one revision with the ApiRevision of 1.

Listing 5-2 uses the Azure PowerShell cmdlet Get-AzApiManagementApiRevision to demonstrate this. It uses the new version of the Demo Conference API conf-api-v1.

Listing 5-2. Get all revisions of an API.

```
Get-AzApiManagementApiRevision `
    -Context $apimContext `
    -ApiId conf-api-v1
```

Let us now create a new revision and see how we can call it.

Add a New Revision

Revisions share the same API identifier (ApiId) in the sense that you provide the same identifier for all revisions as a parameter. As you will see after you have created a new revision, the API identifier has slightly changed. In the following example, you will use the Azure PowerShell cmdlet New-AzApiManagementApiRevision to create a new revision. It has four parameters:

- Context for identifying the instance of Azure API Management.

- ApiId which identifies the API that you will create a new revision of.

- ApiRevision which can be a numeric value or a string.

- SourceApiRevision which identifies the revision you want to copy from. Without this parameter, you would get a revision without any operations.

```
New-AzApiManagementApiRevision `
    -Context $apimContext `
    -ApiId conf-api-v1 `
    -ApiRevision 2 `
    -SourceApiRevision 1
```

After you have executed this cmdlet, you will have two revisions that can be individually changed and tested in any way. An API consumer would still hit revision 1 unless it is called by adding the following string to the URL ;rev=2. The complete URL would like this: *https://mastering-apim.azure-api.net/conf/v1;rev=2/topics*. As mentioned previously, the API identifier has changed slightly. Running the cmdlet of Listing 5-2 will return two revisions, one with the API identifier conf-api-v1 and the other conf-api-v1;rev=2.

In the following section, you will learn how to make revision 2 as the current revision where an API consumer won't need to add the revision number ;rev=2.

Make Revision Current

At some point, when you have developed and tested a new revision, you want your API consumers to call it without being specific in the URL. You can do this by making a revision as *current*. The Azure PowerShell cmdlet for this is New-AzApiManagementApiRelease. It requires the context, ApiId, and ApiRevision parameters.

```
New-AzApiManagementApiRelease `
    -Context $apimContext `
    -ApiId conf-api-v1 `
    -ApiRevision 2
```

Now that revision is flagged as current, it can be called without specifying the revision number, as this URL demonstrates: https://mastering-apim.azure-api.net/conf/v1/topics.

Summary

In this chapter, you learned how to use API versions and revisions in the context of Azure API Management. This concept is often overseen by developers who simply want to deploy their APIs to Azure API Management. They end up creating a new API with a slightly different path using a suffix such as -v2. The new path of the *not-so-new* API – same API but a new version – is /conf-v2, which results then in the URL https://mastering-apim.azure-api.net/conf-v2/topics.

A good practice of using the concept of versions and revisions in Azure API Management is by including it as part of an API deployment pipeline or routine that you as the Azure API Management engineer or administrator provide to the developers, so they don't have to know these details of Azure API Management.

CHAPTER 6

Subscriptions

An important part of managing APIs in Azure API Management is to govern their usage. In some cases, an API will be open for the public and can be called by anyone and from any client without any restrictions, like the original Demo Conference API that you imported early on. In other cases, you might want to be specific about who can call what API. This is where subscriptions come into play.

Subscriptions describe the APIs that a user can call by including a subscription key in the request. Furthermore, subscription keys can be used within policies to restrict or change the behavior of APIs. In this chapter, you will learn how to manage subscriptions with Azure PowerShell and understand how subscriptions fit into the context of API security. Before we start, let us first take a look at how subscriptions fit into the bigger picture of Azure API Management.

Figure 6-1 shows how subscriptions relate to users, products, and APIs. Both, products and APIs, can be configured in a way that they require a caller to include a subscription key to the request. As users might want to call many APIs across many products, many subscriptions might be associated to a single user. Products on the other side can also be associated to many subscriptions because many users might want to use the same product. Compared to APIs, products allow for an upper limit of subscriptions. Since Azure API Management introduced the consumption pricing tier, a subscription can also be associated with either one or all APIs, which means a product is not a requirement for using subscriptions.

© Sven Malvik 2022
S. Malvik, *Mastering Azure API Management*, https://doi.org/10.1007/978-1-4842-8011-9_6

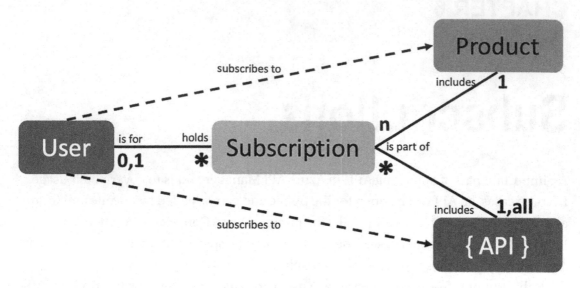

Figure 6-1. *Relation between users, products, APIs, and subscriptions*

Let us look at what subscriptions already exist in your Azure API Management instance by using the Azure PowerShell cmdlet Get-AzApiManagementSubscription and then piping the result for printing some of the attributes. Obtain the context of your Azure API Management instance from Listing 3-5.

```
Get-AzApiManagementSubscription -Context $apimContext | `
    Select-Object SubscriptionId,Name,ProductId,UserId
```

If you have followed the examples in this book, you will get a list of three subscriptions, as shown in Table 6-1. The **Master** subscription is the only subscription that can't be deleted. As its name suggests, it is a built-in all-access subscription that you should never share. It was introduced to simplify API testing. The other two subscriptions are each associated with a product and the administrator user. They were automatically created when you created the products.

Table 6-1. *Example list of subscriptions*

SubscriptionId	Name	ProductId	UserId
Master	Built-in all-access subscription		
607d4035d613890b4497801b		shopping-service	1
607d4036d613890b4497801d		administrator-service	1

Before we continue and use one of the subscriptions in a request, let us create one subscription in the following section.

Creating a Subscription

You saw in Figure 6-1 that you do not need to associate a user to a subscription. However, you might want to know what user is calling what API. Maybe it is important to you for statistical reasons or because you intend to monetize your APIs. Whatever your reason is, it can be a good idea to have user-specific subscriptions, so you are able to suspend specific users if you must.

You create a subscription with the Azure PowerShell cmdlet New-AzApiManagementSubscription. Besides the context of your Azure API Management instance that you want to use (see Listing 3-5), I set the following parameters:

- SubscriptionId is an identifier that you can choose yourself.

- Name is displayed in the developer portal and often the same as the SubscriptionId.

- ProductId is the product a user can use by this subscription.

- UserId is the user that is identified in a request.

- State can be "Suspended," "Active," "Expired," "Submitted," "Rejected," "Cancelled."

```
New-AzApiManagementSubscription `
    -Context $apimContext `
    -SubscriptionId jon-falk-0815_shopping-service `
    -Name jon-falk-0815_shopping-service `
    -ProductId shopping-service `
    -UserId jon-falk-0815 `
    -State Active
```

When you execute this cmdlet, you will add a new subscription that user Jon Falk can use to call APIs that are associated with the Shopping Service. Let us see how we can do this in the following section.

Revealing Subscription Keys

You will now send a request by using the subscription that you just created. Before you do this, I want to briefly talk about subscription keys that come with a subscription.

Subscriptions come always with two keys, a primary key and a secondary key. Both keys work in the same way, and you can use either of them. The reason there are two of them is in case you must regenerate a key. A user or a client application can simply try the other key.

Listing 6-1 shows how to reveal the subscription keys that you created for Jon Falk by using the Azure PowerShell cmdlet Get-AzApiManagementSubscriptionKey. This cmdlet expects at least two parameters, the context (see Listing 3-5) and the identifier of the subscription.

Listing 6-1. Reveal subscription keys.

```
Get-AzApiManagementSubscriptionKey `
    -Context $apimContext `
    -SubscriptionId jon-falk-0815_shopping-service
```

If you have followed the examples in this book, you won't have an API in the shopping service that you can call. Import therefore the Petstore API and add it to the shopping-service product as shown in the following:

```
#Import API
Import-AzApiManagementApi `
    -Context $apimContext `
    -ApiId petstore-api `
    -SpecificationFormat "OpenApiJson" `
    -SpecificationUrl "https://petstore.swagger.io/v2/swagger.json" `
    -Path "petstore"

# Add API to product
Add-AzApiManagementApiToProduct `
    -Context $apimContext `
    -ApiId petstore-api `
    -ProductId shopping-service
```

As a last step, I recommend renaming the subscription key that you will send in the header, so it is not obvious to others what API management tool you are using. The default key for a header is `Ocp-Apim-Subscription-Key` and for a query parameter `subscription-key`. Execute the Azure PowerShell cmdlet `Set-AzApiManagementApi` to rename the subscription header key to **ApiKey**.

```
Set-AzApiManagementApi `
    -Context $apimContext `
    -ApiId petstore-api `
    -SubscriptionKeyHeaderName ApiKey
```

Calling API with Subscription Key

As you have all the necessary entities such as user, product, API, and subscription set up, let us look at Figure 6-2 and see how they relate to each other in detail. The Petstore API is associated to the Shopping Service product that the user Jon Falk has subscribed to. He can now use one of the subscription keys to call an operation of the Petstore API.

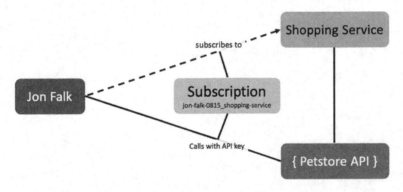

Figure 6-2. *User Jon Falk subscribes to Shopping Service product to call Petstore API with the ApiKey*

Use the following cURL command to call the `/petstore/store/inventory` operation within the Petstore API. Use the primary key that you revealed in Listing 6-1 and replace it with `<PrimaryKey>`.

```
curl -iH "ApiKey: <PrimaryKey>" https://mastering-api-management.azure-api.net/petstore/store/inventory
```

If everything went well, you should get an HTTP status code 200.

Summary

In this chapter, you have learned about the concept of subscriptions in Azure API Management. You understand now how they relate to users, products, and APIs, but also how you create and manage them with Azure PowerShell.

You might assume that subscription keys contribute to the overall security of the backend APIs as users can get individual subscription keys that only they know about. This is partly true and partly wrong.

Firstly, subscription keys are sent in plaintext, which makes them vulnerable to man-in-the-middle attacks. Secondly, in many organizations that I have seen, Azure API Management is a shared instance. Developers across many different teams and units have access to the same instance and can reveal all subscription keys. As many cyberattacks come from the inside, subscription keys might easily be accessible. They are also observable in logs to those that have access.

Treat subscription keys to govern what API consumers can access what APIs, but not to secure your backend web services. Those should ideally have their own security concepts implemented.

CHAPTER 7

Policies and Named Values

In the previous chapters, we focused on how to manage APIs, products, users, groups, and subscriptions. While all these entities are necessary for describing who can call what API, we have not talked about how Azure API Management can help to alter the behavior of an API. Let me give you three examples of why this might be interesting for you:

- **API migration**: Instead of sending all petstore requests to the same legacy petstore backend API, you might want to send the requests of one operation to a new and modern Azure Function App that you have created.

- **XML to JSON**: You have a legacy web service that sends XML responses, and you use Azure API Management to convert those XML responses to JSON before returning them to the API consumer.

- **Logging to Event Hub**: You want to log all API calls to Azure Event Hub so that you are more flexible in terms of the consumers of the logs.

As policies are very flexible, and you will learn why in the following sections, the use cases are endless. I like to say that policies are the heart of Azure API Management. It is where you can change the behavior of one operation, an entire API, a product that is affecting many APIs, or all of them.

Named Values in comparison are the properties of the policies and being used within. They are managed independently because they can be used in all policies.

In this chapter, you will learn how to change the behavior of your APIs. We will start by discussing policies from a high level before we make some minor changes to an

© Sven Malvik 2022
S. Malvik, *Mastering Azure API Management*, https://doi.org/10.1007/978-1-4842-8011-9_7

API. You will then learn how to scope a policy to a certain API operation, API, product, or all APIs. Finally, we will look at some policy examples, some are more common; others are more interesting.

Policies

With Azure API Management policies, we can change the behavior of any API. Instead of just accepting an incoming request and routing it to the right backend web service, we can validate the request first and check whether it has the correct headers, we can reply with an alternative response message in case a backend web service does not work as expected, or we can return a result from a cache; the possibilities are endless. The reason for this flexibility is policy expressions that we can apply on a request and the response by using a subset of .NET Framework types which we express in the *C#* language. Azure API Management provides already many predefined policy statements such as validating the content, setting usage quota, or rewriting URLs. Those predefined policy statements are expressed in *XML*. Before we dive into a policy and implement a behavioral change in an API, let us first understand the inner working of a policy.

You might ask yourself, why should I want to code in C# within XML. The simple answer is: "You don't." Microsoft bought this service with this concept already in place and as of now, there are no plans to change this. Obviously, this is a drawback of Azure API Management. However, there are utilities that help you to implement policies that you will learn about.

Figure 7-1 shows an API consumer (Client) that sends a request to an API with a policy. The policy describes four sections. Behavioral changes that you will make on an incoming request goes into the **inbound** section. You might remember when you mocked an API operation (see Figure 3-2), you did this in the inbound section of the policy.

Changes can also be made right before a request is being forwarded to the backend web service. Later in this chapter, you will learn how to change the backend web service of an API operation in the **backend** section of a policy.

Before you send a response back to the client, you might want to make a behavioral change there as well. As an example, you might need to add a certain header to all responses across all APIs. Maybe you want to transform an XML response from a certain legacy web service into JSON. You do this in the **outbound** section of a policy.

Finally, whenever an error occurs, like a timeout from a backend web service, you can catch this in the **on-error** section and add a good and consistent error message across all APIs to the response.

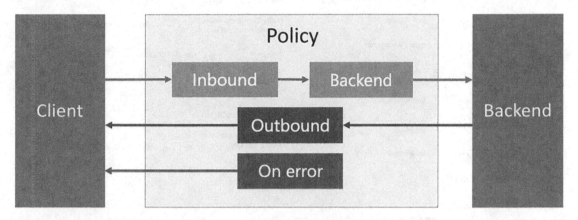

Figure 7-1. *Policy statements and expressions flow*

What you have seen now is how one policy works from a high-level perspective. What you have not seen and learned yet is how to implement a policy and how to scope a policy to what operation, API, or product you want. Before we discuss each of these questions, let us look at a default policy from the inside, the XML code.

Simple Policy

In this section, I will show you a policy from the inside, talk about the XML code, and implement a minor behavioral change; limiting the rate that an API can be called. Before you continue and implement this, let us look at a default policy by navigating to the policy editor in the Azure portal for one API operation, as shown in Figure 7-2.

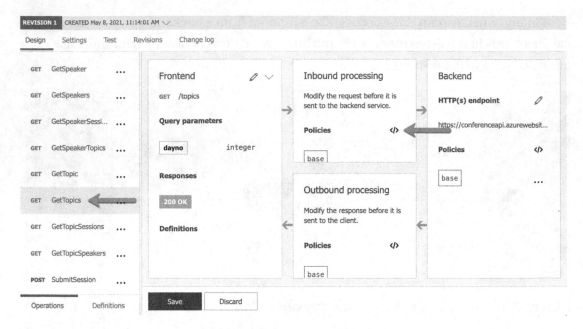

Figure 7-2. *Navigating to the policy editor*

You will now see the policy editor for the *GetTopics* endpoint. Listing 7-1 shows the default policy that describes the implementation of Figure 7-1. It shows the four sections, inbound, backend, outbound, and on-error. Within these sections, you find the `<base />` definition which inserts a policy that is scoped one level above. We will discuss scoping in the following section. For now, pretend that it is not there, as we will only deal with one policy in this section.

Listing 7-1. Default policy

```
<policies>
    <inbound>
        <base />
    </inbound>
    <backend>
        <base />
    </backend>
    <outbound>
        <base />
    </outbound>
```

```
<on-error>
    <base />
</on-error>
</policies>
```

The default policy does not change behavior in any way. We will change this now by adding the predefined policy statement `<rate-limit-by-key>` to the inbound section as Listing 7-2 shows. The attributes tell that we can call the *GetTopics* operation five times (`calls`) within one minute (`renewal-period`). The numbers are based on a key (`counter-key`) which is an IP address that is stored in `context.Request.IpAddress`. We will dive into the syntax and expressions in a later section.

Listing 7-2. Limiting the number of calls per IP address

```
<inbound>
    <base />
    <rate-limit-by-key calls="5" renewal-period="60" counter-key="@
    (context.Request.IpAddress)" />
</inbound>
```

After clicking **Save**, you can test this policy by calling the *GetTopics* operation six times. I used a simple for-loop in *Bash* and printed only the HTTP status code separated with a comma.

```
for i in $(seq 1 6); do
    curl -s -o /dev/null -w "%{http_code}," -H "ApiKey: <YOUR_SUBSCRIPTION_
    KEY>" https://mastering-apim.azure-api.net/conf/topics
done
```

The result is as expected; it went well five times before we received the HTTP status code 429 (Too many requests). Remember that the policy is based on the IP address. Clients with other IP addresses can still call this operation and receive an HTTP status code 200 (OK).

```
200,200,200,200,200,429
```

You have learned how to change a policy on API operation level by making a simple change in the policy editor of the Azure portal. In the following section, you will learn how to scope policies for operations, APIs, products, and all APIs.

Scoping

Policies can be scoped on different levels, global, product, API, and operation. They can be mixed or stand-alone. In the previous section, you implemented a change in a policy of one operation. You noticed the policy statement `<base />`. It tells where an upper-level policy will be inserted. Before we will implement an example to demonstrate this, let us look at how policies depend on each other

Figure 7-3 shows a global policy at the top that *can* be inserted in all policies in the levels that are below. I say "can" because it depends on whether you set `<base />` or not, and so, will be inserted in a policy below or not. The same is true for all other policies. At the end, you will have an effective policy that might include a combination of policies from each level. I marked policies on each level with a star to highlight those that would be part of an effective policy.

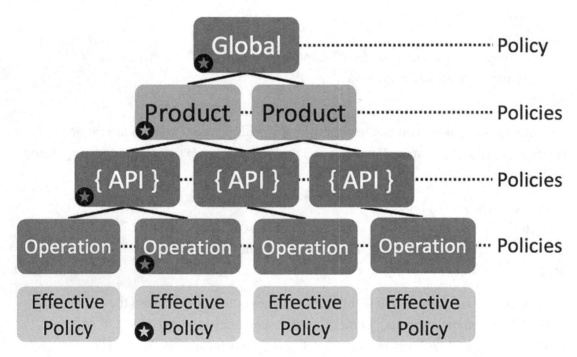

Figure 7-3. *Policy scoping*

You learned where to implement a policy for an operation. As there is a policy on each level, I want to show you where to access the other policies in the Azure portal.

Figure 7-4 shows where to click in the Azure portal to access the policy editor for each level despite the product level policy. You find the policy editor for products by selecting a product in the Azure portal and then clicking **Policies**. We will deploy policies in a different way in a later chapter.

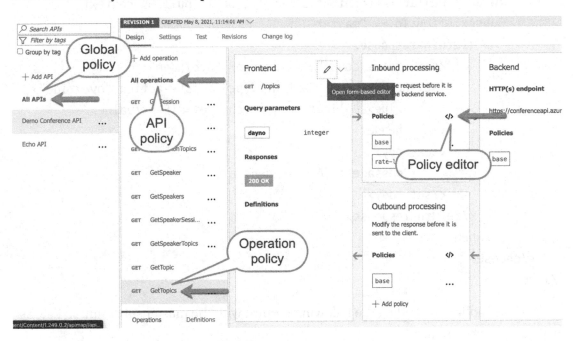

Figure 7-4. *Policies in different scopes*

You will now implement a policy on the global level and prevent the use of the `master` subscription key "Built-in-all-access subscription" for all calls no matter what product, API, or operation is called. This can be useful to prevent calls that accidentally have been shared with your API consumers as this key allows access to all operations in Azure API Management.

Click on **All APIs** and then open the policy editor as shown in Figure 7-4. Replace then the inbound section of this global policy with the code from Listing 7-3. The implementation uses a control flow policy that is expressed with `<choose/>`. We will discuss syntax and expressions in the following section. Inside the `<choose/>` element, you must put at least one `<when/>` element with a condition. In this example, we check whether the subscription is set and its **Id** equal's "master". If both evaluations are true, we create a new response by setting the HTTP status code to 400 (Bad Request), the `Content-Type` header to json, and the body with a message saying "Access denied."

Listing 7-3. Deny policy for the master subscription key

```
<inbound>
    <choose>
        <when condition="@(context.Subscription != null && context.
        Subscription.Id == "master")">
            <return-response>
                <set-status code="403" reason="Forbidden" />
                <set-header name="Content-Type" exists-action="override">
                    <value>application/json;charset=UTF-8</value>
                </set-header>
                <set-body>
                    {"message": "Access denied."}
                </set-body>
            </return-response>
        </when>
    </choose>
</inbound>
```

Test this policy by sending the following request with the master subscription key, as Listing 7-4 demonstrates.

Listing 7-4. Calling an API with the master subscription key

```
curl -iH "ApiKey: <MASTER_SUBSCRIPTION_KEY>" https://mastering-apim.azure-
api.net/conf/topics
```

If everything went well, you should receive the following response:

```
HTTP/1.1 403 Forbidden
Content-Length: 75
Content-Type: application/json;charset=UTF-8
Date: Sat, 08 May 2021 16:12:25 GMT
{"message": "Access denied."}
```

You have implemented two policies, one on the operational level for *GetTopics* and one on the global level. The response was an **Access denied** message. What happens if we send the same request six times? You remember that the policy of the *GetTopics* operation will return an HTTP status code 429. The answer to this question is in the following section.

Calculating Effective Policy

As you implement policies on different levels, you might lose track of what an effective policy would look like. An effective policy is a complete policy that includes policies from all levels, global, product, API, and operation. In Listings 7-2 and 7-3, you implemented two policies, one for an operation and then the global policy.

Figure 7-5 shows how to calculate the effective policy for an operation that a request would call. Click **Calculate effective policy**. A list with all available products will appear. As you can implement policies on product level as well, you will select the product that the user you want to test with would use.

Figure 7-5. *Calculate effective policy*

As a result of the calculation, an effective policy will appear as Listing 7-5 shows. I show only the inbound section of the effective policy here because we have not changed any other section (`backend`, `outbound`, `on-error`) yet. The policy shows that the global policy got inserted before the operation policy. Sending the same request (see Listing 7-4) six times will always return HTTP status code 400, never 429. You can change this by changing the sequence and setting `<rate-limit-by-key>` before `<base/>` of Listing 7-2. As mentioned earlier, `<base/>` inserts the upper-level policy (see Figure 7-3). If you remove `<base/>`, the upper-level policy won't be inserted at all.

Listing 7-5. Effective policy

```
<inbound>
    <!-- base: Begin Api scope -->
    <!-- base: Begin Product scope -->
    <!-- base: Begin Global scope -->
    <choose>
        <when condition="@(context.Subscription != null && context.
        Subscription.Id == "master")">
            <return-response>
                <set-status code="400" reason="Bad Request" />
                <set-header name="Content-Type" exists-action="override">
                    <value>application/json;charset=UTF-8</value>
                </set-header>
                <set-body>{"message": "Access denied."}</set-body>
            </return-response>
        </when>
    </choose>
    <!-- base: End Global scope -->
    <!-- base: End Product scope -->
    <!-- base: End Api scope -->
    <rate-limit-by-key calls="5" renewal-period="60" counter-key=
    "@(context.Request.IpAddress)" />
</inbound>
```

You have now learned how policies on different levels depend on each other and how to calculate an effective policy. Even though that you have implemented just a few lines of code in two policies, the effective policy has many lines, and it might get harder to maintain policies without tools that can help us to manage them. Imagine how an effective policy would look like if you had implemented a policy with several expressions on each level. We will dive into how to work with policies in a later chapter.

Expressions

An expression within a policy is well-formed C# code that has access to the implicitly provided context variable and a subset of .NET Framework types. Before we look at the context variable and the .NET Framework types, I want to show you how to write expressions in Azure API Management policies.

There are two types of statement expressions, single statement expressions and multi-statement expressions. Let us discuss each of them in the following two sections by using some examples.

Single Statement Expressions

Single statement expressions are enclosed in @(expression). You have already seen some examples like in the example with rate-limit-by-key from Listing 7-2, where we read the requester's IP address.

```
<rate-limit-by-key calls="5" renewal-period="60" counter-key="@(context.
Request.IpAddress)" />.
```

Another example of a single statement expression is assigning a value to a variable with set-value. Let us assume that we need a certain value like the requester's IP address at several places within an effective policy, meaning that we need the IP address across several policy scopes, as shown in Figure 7-3. We can set the IP address in the inbound section of *GetTopics* of the Demo Conference API as a single statement expression.

```
<set-variable name="ip" value="@(context.Request.IpAddress)" />
```

Values are bound to the context variable. This means that we have access to them across all scopes of policies. Let us try this out by setting a new header in the outbound section of the global policy – which is a different scope – with the value of the ip variable that we just have set.

```
<outbound>
    <set-header name="X-IP" exists-action="override">
        <value>@((string)context.Variables["ip"])</value>
    </set-header>
    <base />
</outbound>
```

The effective policy will look as is shown in Listing 7-6.

Listing 7-6. Variables in policies

```
<policies>
    <inbound>
        <!-- base: Begin Api scope -->
        <!-- base: Begin Product scope -->
        <!-- base: Begin Global scope -->
        <choose>
            <when condition="@(context.Subscription != null && context.
            Subscription.Id == "master")">
                <return-response>
                    <set-status code="400" reason="Bad Request" />
                    <set-header name="Content-Type" exists-
                    action="override">
                        <value>application/json;charset=UTF-8</value>
                    </set-header>
                    <set-body>{"message": "Access denied."}</set-body>
                </return-response>
            </when>
        </choose>
        <!-- base: End Global scope -->
        <!-- base: End Product scope -->
        <!-- base: End Api scope -->
        <set-variable name="ip" value="@(context.Request.IpAddress)" />
        <rate-limit-by-key calls="5" renewal-period="60" counter-key=
        "@((string)context.Variables["ip"])" />
    </inbound>
    <backend>
        <!-- base: Begin Api scope -->
        <!-- base: Begin Product scope -->
        <!-- base: Begin Global scope -->
        <forward-request />
        <!-- base: End Global scope -->
        <!-- base: End Product scope -->
        <!-- base: End Api scope -->
    </backend>
```

```
<outbound>
    <!-- base: Begin Api scope -->
    <set-header name="X-IP" exists-action="override">
        <value>@((string)context.Variables["ip"])</value>
    </set-header>
    <!-- base: End Api scope -->
</outbound>
<on-error />
</policies>
```

You can now send a request with cURL and print out only the headers to verify that it contains the X-IP header.

```
curl -I -X GET -H "ApiKey: <MASTER_SUBSCRIPTION_KEY>" https://mastering-
apim.azure-api.net/conf/topics
```

Multi-Statement Expressions

Multi-statement expressions are enclosed in @{expressions}. They must end with a return statement where return null; is a valid statement.

In Listing 7-7, I added a multi-statement expression to the inbound section of the "Add a new pet to the store" POST operation of the petstore API from Chapter 6. The operation expects a JSON body with a name of the new pet. The example reads the name and returns it as plaintext. We will use the return-response definition and set the pet's name in the body with set-body.

Listing 7-7. Multi-statement expression

```
<inbound>
    <return-response>
        <set-body>@{
            JObject body = context.Request.Body.As<JObject>();
            return (string)body["name"];
        }</set-body>
    </return-response>
    <base />
</inbound>
```

You can test it by sending a POST request with a JSON string, as Listing 7-8 demonstrates.

Listing 7-8. Calling POST operation

```
curl -X POST \
    -d "{\"name\": \"Sina the dog}]}" \
    -iH "ApiKey: <MASTER_SUBSCRIPTION_KEY>" \
    -H "Content-Type: application/json" \
    https://mastering-apim.azure-api.net/petstore/pet
```

The response will be `Sina`.

```
HTTP/1.1 200 OK
Content-Length: 4
Date: Sat, 15 May 2021 13:17:21 GMT
Sina
```

This example demonstrated how you can implement policies over multiple lines. Be aware that multi-statement expressions lead to larger effective policies. Implementing larger policies on different scope levels can become harder to maintain over time, especially if you have many API developers that work within the same instance of Azure API Management. I have seen effective policies over many hundreds of lines. Maintaining those can become very challenging. Luckily, there are tools that can help us and that give us debugging capabilities. We will discuss this in a later chapter.

Named Values

Named values are key/value pairs that are used in policies. Instead of using hard coded values in policies that might change over time, we can set placeholders (named values) that can be changed independently from policies. There are three different types of them, plaintext, secrets, and Azure Key Vault secrets.

Plaintext

Until now, we have routed our requests to the original backend APIs. In case of the petstore API, our requests were routed to `https://petstore.swagger.io/v2`. Let us now assume that we forked and changed the petstore backend API. Instead of calling the old backend API at petstore.swagger.io, we will route all petstore requests to a new URL https://petstore.azurecloud.no, as shown in Listing 7-9. We can do this by using set-backend-service in the inbound section of the API policy.

Listing 7-9. Route request to backend API

```
<inbound>
    <base />
    <set-backend-service base-url="https://petstore.azurecloud.no" />
</inbound>
```

Let us also assume that we are working on a new implementation of the petstore API and we want to change the URL in the API policy. In such a case you use named values.

Figure 7-6 visualizes the use case that we are going to implement in Azure API Management. All clients call the petstore API by using the URL of Azure API Management https://mastering-apim.azure-api.net/petstore. The API policy of the petstore API changes from https://petstore.swagger.io to https://petstore. azurecloud.no, as shown in Listing 7-9. We also know that we will change the URL again, to a new backend API https://store.azurecloud.no.

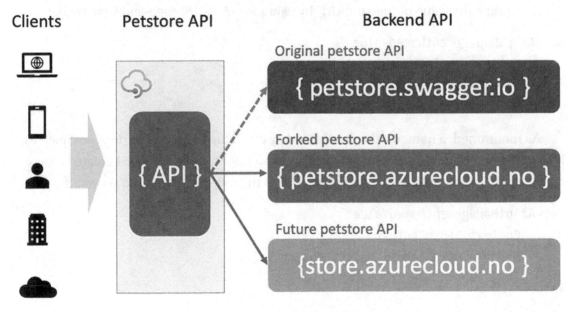

Figure 7-6. *Routing to different backend APIs*

Instead of hard coding the URL of our forked petstore API `https://petstore.` `azurecloud.no` in the API policy, we will use a named value that we can change independently from policies, which simplifies the process of changing the backend URL to a future petstore API.

You can use a named value by replacing the URL with the key "petstoreUrl" inside two curly brackets.

```
<set-backend-service base-url="{{petstoreUrl}} " />
```

If you click **Save**, it will fail. The reason is that the **petstoreUrl** named value does not exist yet. Create a new named value with the Azure PowerShell cmdlet `New-AzApiManagementNamedValue`. Remember to set the `$apimContext` variable first by executing the code from Listing 3-5.

```
New-AzApiManagementNamedValue `
    -Context $apimContext `
    -Name petstoreUrl `
    -NamedValueId petstoreUrl `
    -Value https://petstore.azurecloud.no
```

Once the future petstore API is implemented and you want to route all calls, you can simply update the value of "petstoreUrl" by using `Set-AzApiManagementNamedValue`.

```
Set-AzApiManagementNamedValue `
    -Context $apimContext `
    -NamedValueId petstoreUrl `
    -Value https://store.azurecloud.no
```

As mentioned, a named value is replaced by the value of it. A value does not need to be a string or a number; it can contain policy expressions, code, as well. I created a new named value **code** that has the value **100+100** as the following example shows.

```
Get-AzApiManagementNamedValue `
    -Context $apimContext `
    -NamedValueId code | Select-Object Value
```

```
Value
-----
100+100
```

In Listing 7-10, I replaced the inbound section of the "Add a new pet to the store" policy, where I set a variable `calculatedValue` with the value of `{{code}}`. Sending the same request of Listing 7-8 will result in **200**.

Listing 7-10. Code as Named Value

```
<return-response>
    <set-body>@{
        int calculatedValue = {{code}};
        return calculatedValue.ToString();
    }</set-body>
</return-response>
```

Setting the value of a named value to C# code is possible. However, it is something that you should avoid doing as maintaining such a policy can get difficult.

Secrets

We have worked with plaintext values in the previous section. In this section, we will work with secrets, encrypted values. Secrets are managed in a slightly different way than plaintext values. Let us first create a secret by executing the `New-AzApiManagementNamedValue` cmdlet once again. This time, we add a new parameter `-Secret` which tells Azure API Management to encrypt this value.

```
New-AzApiManagementNamedValue `
    -Context $apimContext `
    -Name mysecret `
    -NamedValueId mysecret `
    -Value "TOP SECRET" `
    -Secret
```

As secrets are encrypted named values, they must be accessed with a different PowerShell cmdlet, `Get-AzApiManagementNamedValueSecretValue`. Executing the following cmdlet will decrypt the value.

```
Get-AzApiManagementNamedValueSecretValue `
    -Context $apimContext `
    -NamedValueId mysecret | Select-Object Value
```

```
Value
-----
TOP SECRET
```

Listing 7-11 shows a modified example of Listing 7-10 of the inbound section where we return the secret.

Listing 7-11. Secret in policy

```
<return-response>
    <set-body>@{
        return "{{mysecret}}";
    }</set-body>
</return-response>
```

Sending the same POST request from Listing 7-8 will result in **TOP SECRET**.

```
curl -X POST \
    -d "{\"name\": \"Sina the dog}]}" \
    -iH "ApiKey: <SUBSCRIPTION_KEY>" \
    -H "Content-Type: application/json" \
    https://mastering-apim.azure-api.net/petstore/pet
```

Another example where secrets are used is by importing an Azure Logic App and using Azure API Management as the API gateway. In such a case, the shared access signature of the Logic App is stored as a secret and used in a `rewrite-uri` policy definition of the operation.

Secrets from Azure Key Vault

Many teams in many organizations share an instance of Azure API Management. This is necessary to bundle APIs to products. The challenge for some organizations might be to protect certain named values such as secrets from developers that have access to the shared instance of Azure API Management but who should not be eligible to access certain secrets. As an example, one team works on a web service and makes it accessible for customers that are already using some other APIs. To protect the web service from being accessed from other channels than Azure API Management, they implemented basic authentication which requires credentials in the header of a request. It's therefore common practice to store secrets not as named values but in an Azure Key Vault.

Figure 7-7 shows how to enable Azure API Management to read secrets from Azure Key Vault by using its managed service identity.

Azure API Management   Managed Identity   Azure Key Vault

Figure 7-7. *Azure API Management uses its identity to access Azure Key Vault*

Let us look at an example by using Azure Key Vault for storing a secret that we will use in the policy of Listing 7-11.

Enable Managed System Identity in Azure API Management

In Azure, a managed system identity can be assigned to a managed resource such as an Azure Function, App Service, and also an instance of Azure API Management. A resource with an identity has the capabilities to work with other resources that leverage Azure Active Directory for authentication. We can enable a managed system identity (MSI) in Azure API management either manually in the Azure portal or by using the Azure PowerShell cmdlet `Set-AzApiManagement` as the following example shows. The cmdlet requires two parameters in our case, an input object and the flag that is saying that you want to enable a system managed identity. The input object is not the context from Listing 3-5 that we have used throughout this book. Instead, it is the name of your instance and the resource group. You can either set both values directly with `Get-AzApiManagement` or read them from the context variable `$apimContext` as shown:

```
$apim = Get-AzApiManagement `
    -Name $apimContext.ServiceName `
    -ResourceGroupName $apimContext.ResourceGroupName

Set-AzApiManagement `
    -InputObject $apim `
    -SystemAssignedIdentity
```

What happens when you enable a system managed identity is that a representation of the Azure API Management instance in the form of an application gets created in Azure Active Directory. It is the application ID, or client ID, that you will need to tell Azure Key Vault to allow access from there, as Figure 7-7 describes.

Figure 7-8 shows how to get the application (client) ID of your Azure API Management instance. Navigate to the left-hand menu or to the search field at the top in the Azure portal to Azure Active Directory. Choose **App registration** or search for the service name, in my case *master-apim*. Copy the value of **Application (client) ID**; you will need this ID in the next section. If you want to learn how MSI works in detail, visit Managed identities for Azure resources | Microsoft Docs.

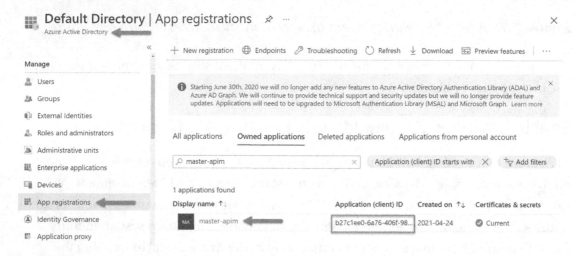

Figure 7-8. *Obtain the application (client) ID of Azure API Management*

You have now prepared Azure API Management for accessing Azure Key Vault. Let us in the next section create first an Azure Key Vault, and then set the right access policy for Azure API Management.

Preparing Azure Key Vault

Until now, we have not yet created an Azure Key Vault. You can do this either by searching for it in the Azure portal or by creating it with Azure PowerShell. As the focus of this book is Azure API Management, we will use the simplest way and use the Azure PowerShell cmdlet `New-AzKeyVault`. The cmdlet requires a name, the location, and the resource group to deploy to, as the following example shows:

```
New-AzKeyVault `
    -Name MasteringApimKeyVault `
    -Location WestEurope `
    -ResourceGroupName mastering-apim-rg
```

You will now have a new Azure Key Vault. Figure 7-9 demonstrates how to add a new secret *mykvsecret*. Click **Generate/import** to create a new secret with a value of your choice; I set it to "TOP SECRET FROM KEY VAULT".

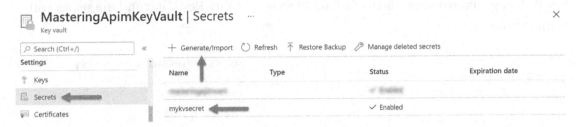

Figure 7-9. *Create secret in Azure Key Vault*

The next step is to authorize Azure API Management to get secrets from this Azure Key Vault. You will do this by setting an access policy for the managed identity you created in the previous section. We will use the Azure PowerShell cmdlet `Set-AzKeyVaultAccessPolicy`. The cmdlet requires the name of your Azure Key Vault and the resource group it is deployed to. Furthermore, you will set the `ServicePrincipalName` to the **Application (client) ID** from Figure 7-8 which represents your Azure API Management instance. Lastly, you will set the access policy to at least *get* and *list,* as the following example demonstrates:

```
Set-AzKeyVaultAccessPolicy `
    -VaultName MasteringApimKeyVault `
    -ResourceGroupName mastering-apim-rg `
    -ServicePrincipalName <Application (client) ID> `
    -PermissionsToSecrets get,list
```

Once executed, Azure API Management is authorized to read secrets from your Azure Key Vault.

Using Secret from Azure Key Vault in Policies

The setup of Figure 7-8 is now in place and it is time to use secrets in policies. In comparison to encrypted values that are stored in Azure API Management, secret values from Azure Key Vault are stored as references in Azure API Management.

Figure 7-10 shows how to add reference to a secret from Azure Key Vault in Azure API Management. Open **Named Values** in the left-hand menu of Azure API Management and click **Add** to create a new named value pair. Give it a name and select the type **Key Vault**. A new plane opens where you will select your Azure Key Vault and the secret you want to reference.

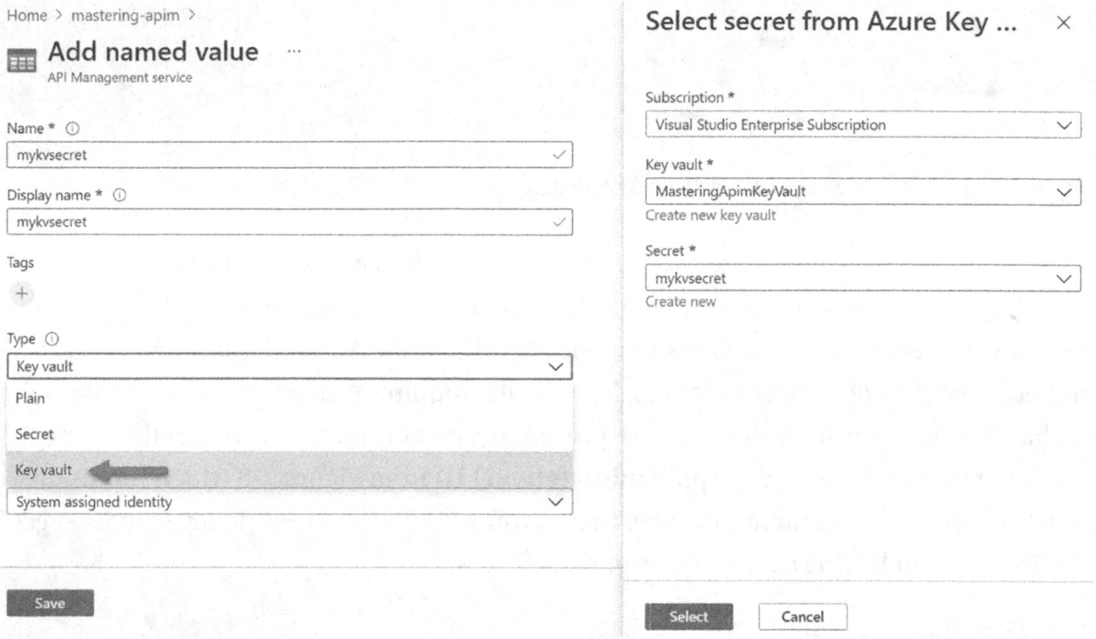

Figure 7-10. *Adding a secret from Azure Key Vault*

Referencing a secret from Azure Key Vault is only possible because you gave it permission by adding an access policy for the managed system identity of your Azure API Management instance.

From here, you can proceed as you did in Listing 7-11. In the following inbound section of the "Add a new pet to the store" policy, I changed only the named value to {{mykvsecret}}, as the following example shows:

```
<return-response>
    <set-body>@{
        return "{{mykvsecret}}";
    }</set-body>
</return-response>
```

Save your change and call this operation by using the following cURL command that you have used before:

```
curl -X POST \
    -d "{\"name\": \"Sina the dog}]}" \
    -iH "ApiKey: <SUBSCRIPTION_KEY>" \
    -H "Content-Type: application/json" \
    https://mastering-apim.azure-api.net/petstore/pet
```

The response of this call will be your secret value, presented in plaintext. In my case, it is **TOP SECRET FROM KEY VAULT**.

Examples

You have learned the essentials of policies in Azure API Management. You also got the tools to create and maintain these policies. In this section, we will look at two interesting use cases and discuss how to implement them in policies.

Validations

We have not discussed security in Azure API Management yet – we will so in a later chapter – however, I want to give you a brief overview and introduce validation policies. Even though validation policies are part of API security, they are not a replacement for a Web Application Firewall (WAF), but they can help to mitigate possible attacks on web APIs.

There are four different validation policies available in Azure API Management, `validate-content`, `validate-parameters`, `validate-headers`, and `validate-status-code`. I will demonstrate the first two in this section as the next two are very similar to implement.

Note   Validation policies may affect API throughput and it is recommended to perform load tests before using them in production. More details about performance implications.

Whatever you will validate, headers, query, or path parameters, there are three different actions to choose from, ignore, prevent, and detect.

Content Validation

The content validation policy validate-content does one thing; it checks the size of the content against the attribute max-size. In the following inbound section of our well-known "Add a new pet to the store" policy, I set the max size to 25 bytes, one byte less than the payload I am going to send "Sina the dog," the name of my dog. Payload that exceeds 25 bytes will result in an HTTP status code 400 (Bad Request) through setting size-exceeded-action to prevent. Setting an action as *prevent* will result in an HTTP status code 400 (Bad Request) and not be forwarded to the backend web service. Furthermore, I set unspecified-content-type-action to *detect,* which will log this event; we will discuss logging in detail in a later chapter.

```
<inbound>
    <validate-content
        max-size="25"
        size-exceeded-action="prevent"
        unspecified-content-type-action="detect"
        errors-variable-name="err" />
    <base />
</inbound>
```

You can try this content validation policy by sending more than 25 bytes in the payload as I did with "Sina the dog."

```
curl -X POST \
    -d "{\"name\": \"Sina the dog}]}" \
    -iH "ApiKey: <SUBSCRIPTION_KEY>" \
    -H "Content-Type: application/json" \
    https://mastering-apim.azure-api.net/petstore/pet
```

The response is an HTTP status code 400 (Bad Request) and a detailed message about this error.

```
{ "statusCode": 400, "message": "Request's body is 25 bytes long and it
exceeds the configured limit of 24 bytes." }
```

Parameter Validation

Another validation policy is parameter validation `validate-parameters`. This policy validates incoming *header*, *query*, and *path* parameters. Before we make any change in the policy itself, I want to show you how to change the API specification in the Azure portal instead of re-importing the API. We will need this to demonstrate the following example.

Figure 7-11 shows where you can change the API specification. In this case, I added several request headers that I expect to receive in any call to this API operation "Add a new pet to the store."

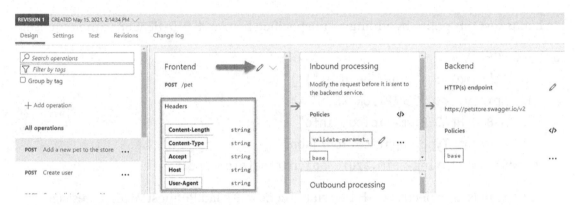

Figure 7-11. *Adding headers to the API specification*

In the following example, I block all requests that contain unspecified headers. Remember that I specified several headers in Figure 7-11. I will ignore these headers by defining `specified-parameter-action="ignore"` in both `validate-parameters` and `headers`. As a note, child definitions overwrite parent definitions which we will do in the next policy definition `unspecified-parameter-action`, which I have set to *prevent*. It means that all headers that are not specified will result in an HTTP status code 400 (Bad Request). The petstore API requires a subscription key so we must allow the ApiKey header. I have set a parameter policy inside the headers policy with the name of the header `ApiKey` and the action *ignore*. We could have added `ApiKey` to the API specification itself. However, this approach would have tightly coupled the web API to Azure API Management.

```
<inbound>
    <validate-parameters
     specified-parameter-action="ignore"
```

```
        unspecified-parameter-action="ignore"
        errors-variable-name="err ">
            <headers
              specified-parameter-action="ignore"
              unspecified-parameter-action="prevent">
                  <parameter name="ApiKey" action="ignore" />
            </headers>
      </validate-parameters>
      <base />
</inbound>
```

Let us test this policy by adding an unspecified header X-BAD-HEADER to the request.

```
curl -X POST \
    -d "{\"name\": \"Sina the dog\"}]}" \
    -H "ApiKey: <SUBSCRIPTION_KEY>" \
    -H "X-BAD-HEADER: malicious info" \
    -H "Content-Type: application/json" \
    https://mastering-apim.azure-api.net/petstore/pet
```

The result is as expected, an HTTP status code 400 (Bad Request) with a message saying that there is an unspecified header.

```
{ "statusCode": 400, "message": "Unspecified header X-BAD-HEADER is not
allowed." }
```

Let us take a quick look at the other two validation policies in the next section.

Other Validations

Even though we have learned how to validate headers, these were for incoming calls only, meaning that they were scoped to the inbound section of all policies. There is a separate validation policy for responses that can be defined in the outbound and on-error section for headers validate-headers.

The fourth and last validation policy is the validate-status-code policy which can also be used in the outbound and on-error section of all policies. This policy may be used to prevent leakage of backend errors, which can contain stack traces.

Canary Backend APIs

The following example might not be a common scenario that we can find in many organizations; however, I think it is an important scenario especially for mission-critical workload that is running on Aure Kubernetes Service (AKS) and where Azure API Management really can show its power.

The AKS documentation says it is a highly available, secure, and fully managed Kubernetes service for deploying and managing containerized applications more easily.

While this might be true for the applications running on AKS themselves, upgrading AKS can put your applications in jeopardy though. There are at least three options you can choose from to upgrade your AKS cluster. In theory, all three options work fine. In practice, we have seen problems with the first option. Let me explain these options in short before we discuss how to use Azure API Management to mitigate eventual risks:

- Upgrade AKS by running the Azure CLI command `az aks upgrade`, which will drain all nodes one by one and upgrade them.

- Use node pools in AKS and upgrade them individually by running the Azure CLI command `az aks nodepool upgrade`.

- Provision a new AKS cluster and migrate your workload.

As this book is about Azure API Management, I will not discuss the challenges of each AKS upgrade option. Instead, I want to mention that upgrades in general can and will fail, and you must keep in mind that an upgrade can and will lead to downtime of the workload running there, partially or completely. If you accept this risk, the first two options are good alternatives as they are cheapest and let you use existing Azure CLI commands.

Figure 7-12 shows how to use Azure API Management to support the third option of upgrading an AKS cluster. In this case, Azure API Management acts as an API façade in front of both AKS clusters, the current active (old) cluster that I highlighted in blue and the new cluster that we want to switch to. Even though a new AKS cluster should go through a regression test, we can use Azure API Management to gradually route the traffic over to the new cluster – in this case 90%/10% – and monitor it and follow the logs for eventual error messages. We call the technique of introducing a new AKS cluster and slowly rolling out the change to a small subset of users before rolling it out to the entire infrastructure and making it available to everybody as **canary release**.

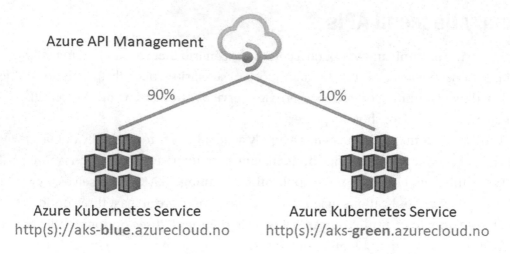

Figure 7-12. *Canary release of Azure Kubernetes Service (AKS)*

In this example, we will focus on steps 3 and 4, testing the workload and switching the traffic from the old, blue AKS cluster over to the new, green AKS cluster. We can do this by implementing a canary release policy in the global policy, so all API calls can use it. The other change we will make is in the API policies where we set the backend URL for the AKS cluster.

Listing 7-12 shows the global policy for a canary release in the *inbound* section. This policy sets a variable aksUrl for the URL of the AKS cluster – blue or green – which is based on a percentage value canaryPercentage that is stored as a named value. It can be gradually changed from 0 to 100 depending on how confident you are with the new AKS cluster. Depending on this value, a variable current-slot is set to either *blue* or *green*. This "slot" is then part of the URL http://aks-(blue|green).azurecloud.no.

Listing 7-12. Global policy for canary release

```
<inbound>
    <choose>
        <when condition="@(new Random().Next(100) < {{canaryPercentage}})">
            <set-variable name="currentSlot" value="{{canarySlot}}" />
        </when>
        <otherwise>
            <set-variable name="currentSlot" value="{{activeSlot}}" />
        </otherwise>
    </choose>
```

```
<set-variable name="aksUrl" value="@("http://aks-" + context.
Variables.GetValueOrDefault<string>("currentSlot", "{{activeSlot}}") +
".azurecloud.no")" />
</inbound>
```

The one task we do in the global policy for the canary release of AKS is setting the URL for AKS as a variable aksUrl. What is missing is setting the URL as the backend service for an operation or an entire API.

Listing 7-13 shows the API policy of *petstore* that we have used throughout this book. It uses the set-backend-service policy of Azure API Management and requires a URL for the base-url attribute. As you can see, variables are stored in the context object. I use the GetValueOrDefault method where I can ensure backward compatibility to a default cluster defaultAKS and then concatenate the context path /petstore.

Listing 7-13. API policy for canary release

```
<set-backend-service base-url="@(context.Variables.
GetValueOrDefault("aksUrl", "{{defaultAKSurl}}") + "/petstore")" />
```

Summary

I hope this chapter gave you a great overview of managing policies in Azure API Management. You learned first the basics of policies and how they are scoped across an operation, an API, products, and all APIs. You saw then how to calculate an effective policy that contains all scopes for a certain operation. You learned then to implement more complex policies by using single- and multi-statement expressions. You embedded placeholders **Named Values** in your policies that you can use across multiple policies. Those Named Values can be in plaintext, secrets, or come from an Azure Key Vault; you tried all three options. Finally, we discussed some examples; some of them are very common, while one of them is not widely used but very interesting as it shows how powerful policies in Azure API Management can be.

As you might have already realized, policies provide almost endless opportunities. This is because we can use a subset of .NET Framework types using C#. However, the drawback is that we must embed our C# code within XML which many developers struggle with and complain about. My advice to this is the following: Keep policies short and simple and implement only what is necessary.

CHAPTER 8

Developer Portal

Throughout this book, we have mostly discussed Azure API Management from the perspective of an administrator and API developer. In this chapter, we will begin by focusing on the API consumers and learn how the default onboarding process works. Of course, the default setup is not necessarily what you want for the organization you will use Azure API Management in. Especially when it comes to corporate branding, you will want to customize the design, texts, and maybe add some more functionality. After we have discussed these topics, you will learn why you might want to host the developer portal yourself instead of letting Azure manage it for you, followed by how you can achieve this.

Overview

Before API consumers can access the developer portal, you must first publish it. You can do this by navigating to `https://<SERVICE_NAME>.developer.azure-api.net/`; in my case, the URL for the developer portal is `https://mastering-apim.developer.azure-api.net/`.

Note The developer portal is not included in the Consumption tier.

It might take some seconds before you will be presented by the administrator view of the developer portal where you can use the WYSIWYG editor – there are other options – to change the design and text. We will customize the developer portal in a later section of this chapter.

Figure 8-1 shows how to publish the developer portal by clicking **Publish website**. This process can take up to 30 seconds.

© Sven Malvik 2022
S. Malvik, *Mastering Azure API Management*, https://doi.org/10.1007/978-1-4842-8011-9_8

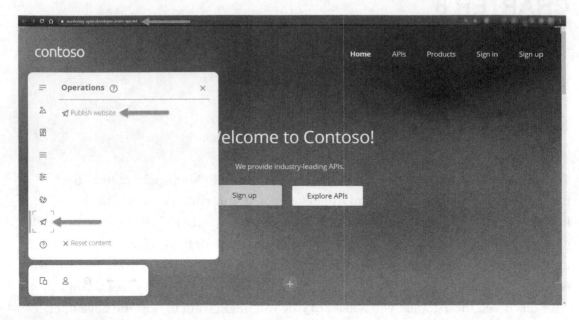

Figure 8-1. *Publishing the developer portal*

I recommend to either log out of Azure or to open a new window in Incognito mode and visit the same IP address again, so you will experience the developer portal from the perspective of a guest API consumer. You might want to navigate around first and find products and APIs that are accessible for the **Guests** user group only as you learned in Chapter 4.

Click **Sign Up** in the upper menu to start the onboarding process by filling out a form with your name, email, and password. This and all following forms can be changed, and we will look at it later in this chapter.

Once you have submitted the *Sign Up* form, you will receive a confirmation email that looks similar to the one shown in Figure 8-2. In the background, Azure API Management will create a new user that is in the *Pending* state.

Please confirm your new private API account

private <apimgmt-noreply@mail.windowsazure.com>   9:34 PM
To sma@azurecloud.no

Quick reply   Reply all   Forward   Delete ≡

Dear Azure Cloud,

Thank you for joining the private API program! We host a growing number of cool APIs and strive to provide an awesome experience for API developers.

First order of business is to activate your account and get you going. To that end, please click on the following link:

https://mastering-apim.developer.azure-api.net/confirm-v2/identities/basic/signup?
userid=60b53a25370337133006a2ce&identity=sma%40azurecloud.no&ticketid=60b53a26370337133006a2d0&ticket=
f45d81bee0a94b84b15ca8a24ec9dbbf

If clicking the link does not work, please copy-and-paste or re-type it into your browser's address bar and hit "Enter".

Thank you,

private API Team

mastering-apim.developer.azure-api.net

Figure 8-2. *Confirmation email for a private API account*

Click the link in the email for confirmation. This process will change the state of your user account from Pending to *Active* and you are ready to subscribe to products.

Figure 8-3 shows the Conferences Services product that I created in a previous chapter. It contains one API, the *Demo Conference API*. You remember that you had to use a subscription key that we called *ApiKey* to call an API. To obtain this key, we must subscribe to the product. Previously, we, as the administrator, have done this directly in the Azure portal. This time, the API consumers themselves can do this by choosing a name and clicking **Subscribe**.

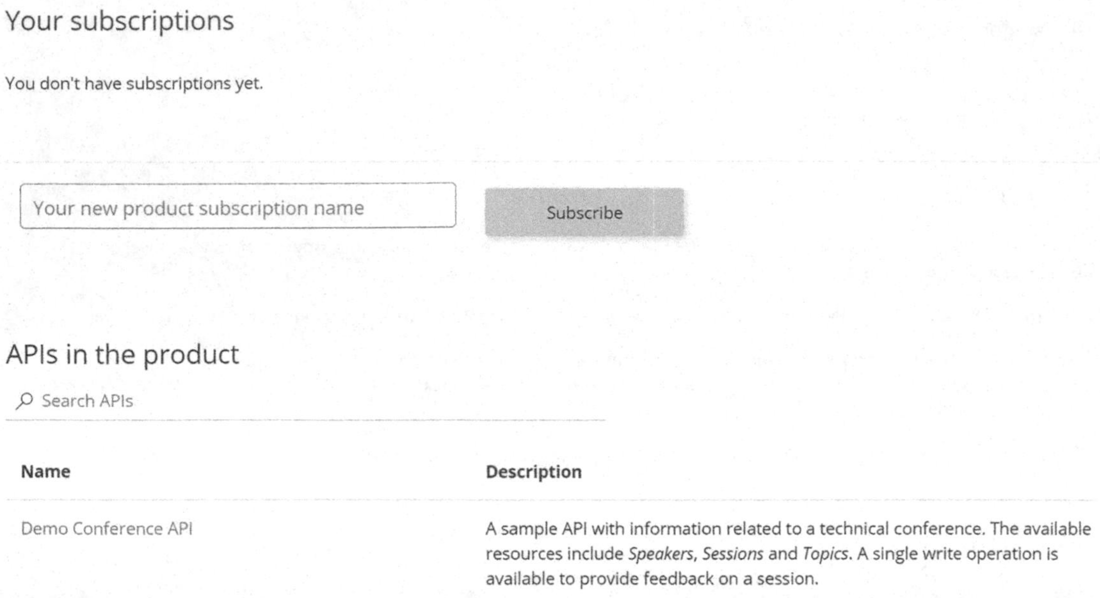

Your subscriptions

You don't have subscriptions yet.

| Your new product subscription name | | Subscribe |

APIs in the product

🔍 Search APIs

Name	Description
Demo Conference API	A sample API with information related to a technical conference. The available resources include *Speakers*, *Sessions* and *Topics*. A single write operation is available to provide feedback on a session.

Figure 8-3. *Subscribing to the Conferences Services product*

The user administration page opens where an API consumer can change its name, password, or even close the account. An API consumer can also reveal the API subscription key. Figure 8-4 shows both keys, the primary subscription key and the secondary subscription key. Make one of them visible by clicking **Show**.

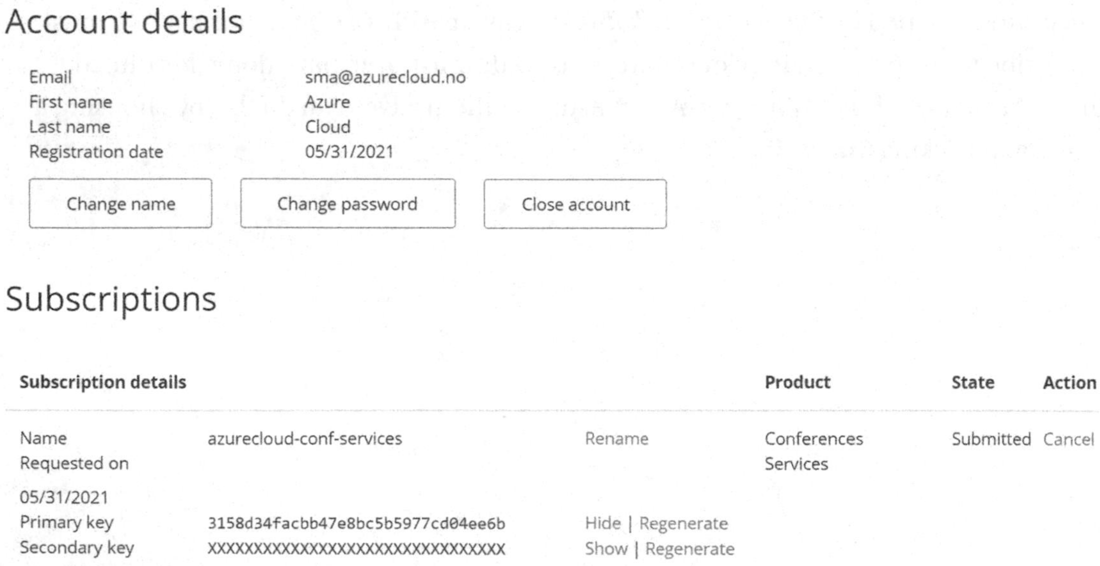

Account details

Email	sma@azurecloud.no
First name	Azure
Last name	Cloud
Registration date	05/31/2021

| Change name | Change password | Close account |

Subscriptions

Subscription details		Product	State	Action
Name	azurecloud-conf-services Rename	Conferences Services	Submitted	Cancel
Requested on				
05/31/2021				
Primary key	3158d34facbb47e8bc5b5977cd04ee6b Hide | Regenerate			
Secondary key	XXXXXXXXXXXXXXXXXXXXXXXXXXXXXXXX Show | Regenerate			

Figure 8-4. *Self-service for the API consumers*

An API consumer can use its API subscription key to call the APIs that are part of the subscribed product. For each product an API consumer wants to subscribe to, a new pair of keys is generated.

Figure 8-5 shows the documentation of the *Demo Conference API* that the API consumer has subscribed. All information you see on this page was extracted from the OpenAPI specification that we imported previously. You *may try* and learn to use this API directly from this documentation by clicking **Try** on the right side. You will then see the same information and fields that you see when you tested this API in the Azure portal. I wrote "may try" as this will not work yet.

Figure 8-5. *Demo Conference API documentation*

As an example, try the `getTopics` operation and use your API subscription key to gain access to it. The response you will get back is *"Since the browser initiates the request, it requires Cross-Origin Resource Sharing (CORS) enabled on the server."* Let us fix this by adding a CORS policy to the global policy.

Figure 8-6 presents a shortcut to enable CORS for all APIs. In case you want to enable CORS for only some APIs or products, I recommend enabling CORS manually.

Figure 8-6. *Enabling CORS for all APIs*

Once you enable CORS for all APIs, a `cors` policy is added to the *inbound* section of the global policy as the following code shows:

```
<inbound>
    <cors allow-credentials="true">
        <allowed-origins>
            <origin>https://mastering-apim.developer.azure-api.net</origin>
        </allowed-origins>
        <allowed-methods preflight-result-max-age="300">
            <method>*</method>
        </allowed-methods>
        <allowed-headers>
            <header>*</header>
        </allowed-headers>
        <expose-headers>
            <header>*</header>
        </expose-headers>
    </cors>
</inbound>
```

In case you want to enable CORS only for some APIs or products, you have two other options. You can either move this code into an API or product policy, or you can enable a CORS proxy for an individual API operation.

Figure 8-7 shows how to enable a CORS proxy for one API operation only. This will route the API calls through the Azure portal's backend in your Azure API Management service and will not need the CORS policy in place.

Figure 8-7. *Enable CORS proxy for an individual API operation*

In the following section, we will focus on making the developer portal our own by customizing its style.

Customization

In this section, you will learn how to customize the developer portal and to make it your own by changing the default style to something unique like a corporate design. There are two ways of customizing the developer portal, by using the built-in WYSIWYG editor or by changing the code of the developer portal templates. In this section, we will focus on the WYSIWYG editor as this is a simple approach that does not require any additional steps. A more complex approach is to change the code of the developer portal templates. This approach requires to host the developer portal by yourself. We will discuss this approach in the following section.

Styling

To customize the developer portal, click **Developer portal** in the upper menu of the
Overview page of your Azure API Management instance. This opens a new tab and
opens the developer portal at `https://<SERVICE_NAME>.developer.azure-api.net/`, in
my case `https://mastering-apim.developer.azure-api.net/`.

I will not go into the details of redesigning the developer portal as this is a very
intuitive and straightforward approach. Instead, I want to show you the first page and
how you can change and remove widgets.

Figure 8-8 shows the WYSIWYG editor of the developer portal. You can change all
texts, pages, images, fonts, and a lot more. Just click on the item you want to change, and
a pen appears. When you click on a pen, a configuration box appears where you can
change the text, image, or what it is that you clicked on. I suggest that you click around at
first. The trash can will remove an item.

Figure 8-8. *Styling the developer portal in the WYSIWYG editor*

To change other pages, click on the link of the page you want to visit while holding
the *Control* key at the same time. Once you are finished, click the save icon below before
you publish the changes, as Figure 8-1 demonstrated.

The developer portal is fully managed by Azure, which means that you do not need
to care about updates.

> **Note** Customizing the *managed* developer portal templates is only possible in the WYSIWYG editor.

In the section about hosting, you will learn another approach of customizing the developer portal where you get full flexibility. Before we dive into the code of the developer portal templates and make changes, let us look at how to change email texts and how to notify important stakeholders by email.

Notifications and Templates

In some cases, it is important to get notified about certain events. Subscription requests that you need to approve is one example; users do not want to wait too long. An email that notifies you as soon as a new subscription request is created will help you to act immediately if necessary. Another example is to get notified when a user closes its account, and you need to do some additional tasks.

Figure 8-9 shows how to add email recipients for different notifications such as for new subscriptions, blind copies, or when a new issue or comment is submitted, which is a feature of the developer portal.

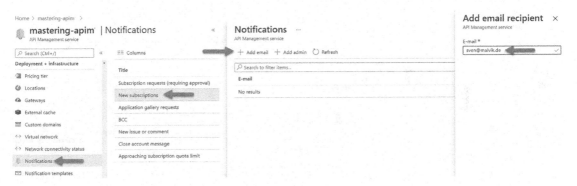

Figure 8-9. *Add email recipients for notifications*

When we created a new API consumer in the developer portal, we received a confirmation email, as shown in Figure 8-2. The sender's email address was apimgmt-noreply@mail.windowsazure.com. Figure 8-10 shows how to change this email address by clicking **E-mail setting** under *Notification templates*. You can also change the name of your organization that appears in the emails.

Figure 8-10. *Change the sender's email address*

Compared to the templates of the managed developer portal, where we must use the WYSIWYG editor – not everyone's favorite editor – we can change the template code of the email notifications directly in the Azure portal, as Figure 8-11 shows. What you see is HTML code, where you can use some variables that will appear on the right-hand side.

Figure 8-11. *Customizing notification email templates*

Another approach of making changes in the code of a notification email template is by cloning and committing changes to the Git repository. You will learn how to work with the Git repository of your Azure API Management instance in a later chapter as there are some side effects that need to be discussed. Also, changes in the code of the Git repository do not apply to the developer portal templates. In such cases, you must host the developer portal yourself, which we will discuss in the following section.

Self-hosting

There are scenarios where you want to make changes in the developer portal that cannot be done in the WYSIWYG editor. It might be the case that you need a custom widget in the developer portal and that is integrated with an internal system of your organization. It might also be the case that you must change the structure of the websites within the developer portal where you need to change the HTML templates. All these changes cannot be done in the WYSIWYG editor or the *portalTemplates* HTML files that you can find in the Git repository of your Azure API Management instance. We will dive into the Git repository in the next chapter.

In this section, you will learn how to host the developer portal in your own environment and make some minor changes. As the developer portal is open source and available on GitHub, it opens the possibility of making changes you need. On the flip side, this comes with the responsibility of hosting, securing, and managing the developer portal on your own.

Running the Developer Portal Locally

Azure provides a detailed step-by-step guide on how to run the developer portal locally. This section will briefly show you how to get started. You will first need a running instance of Azure API Management so the developer portal can connect to it. As the developer portal is a Node.js application, you will need *Node.js* and the package manager *npm*. Download and install Node.js and npm by following the online documentation.

You can find the developer portal on GitHub. Clone the repository with

```
git clone https://github.com/Azure/api-management-developer-portal.git
```

Once you have the repository on your machine, change the directory by running

```
cd api-management-developer-portal
```

Change now from the master branch to the latest release tag of the developer portal. In my case, it is 2.9.0.

```
git checkout 2.9.0
```

Install to download all project dependencies with

```
npm install
```

117

This will take a while. In the meantime, you can open the project in an IDE like Visual Studio Code and configure it so it can connect to your Azure API Management instance.

There are three files you must configure, `config.design.json`, `config.publish.json`, and `config.runtime.json`. Change `<service-name>` in all three files with the name of your Azure API Management instance, in my case "mastering-apim." Furthermore, change "SharedAccessSignature …" with your access token that you can get from the Azure portal, as shown in Figure 8-12. Navigate to **Management API** and click on **Enable Management REST API**. Then, click **Generate** to get an access token that you can copy and replace.

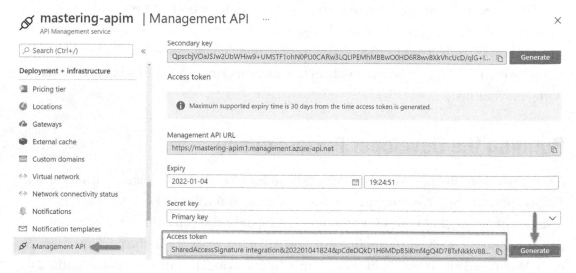

Figure 8-12. *Creating an access token*

To run the developer portal locally, you execute `npm start`. Before we do this, let us make a quick change to see an actual change. I opened the signup.html file `src\components\users\signup\ko\runtime\signup.html` and added a personal string at the beginning of the file.

After I have executed `npm start`, I can access the developer portal on http://localhost:8080 and navigate to *Sign Up*. As Figure 8-13 shows, it contains a new string "HHEELLOO."

Sign up

Already a member? Sign in.

SIGN-UP FORM: BASIC

ΉHEELLOO ◄━━━━━━━━━

Email *

```
e.g. name@example.com
```

Password *

Confirm password *

First name *

```
e.g. John
```

Last name *

```
e.g. Doe
```

Sign up

Figure 8-13. *Minor change in the sign-up form*

Hosting the developer portal by yourself gives you full flexibility. As the developer portal will generate a static web app, you get some options for hosting it. Run the following command to generate the complete static web app of the developer portal:

```
npm publish
```

This will create a new folder ./dist within your project. One option of hosting a static web app is Azure Static Web Apps, which can be integrated with your own GitHub repository of your own version of the developer portal. Another option for hosting a static web app is by using an Azure Storage account and uploading the folder ./dist/website to a blob. We will not dive further into static web apps as it is not contributing to get a better understanding of Azure API Management.

Summary

In this chapter, you learned to administrate the developer portal of Azure API Management but also how you can change the look and feel of it. As the managed developer portal is not fully customizable, you learned then how you can host it yourself, so you are free to fully change its design templates.

PART III

Workflow

## CHAPTER 9

API Development in Context

When I joined the Norwegian payment service Vipps AS three years ago, we were about 30 developers that deployed our web services to Azure Kubernetes Service, AKS. We used already Azure API Management as our API gateway. As we were just a few developers, the number of API changes in a week were just a few. One developer that knew Azure API Management well enough at that time was responsible for maintaining and administrating our two instances, one in the test and one in the production environment. This developer was deploying APIs, creating products, adding named values, and did everything related to these two instances. This worked well three years ago. As the company grew and more developers created more APIs, this developer became a bottleneck. One day, I had worked there for about three months, this developer suddenly left the company. As Azure API Management was a black box for me and most of my co-workers, this was a challenge. As I was eager to learn Azure API Management, I said *Yes*, not to become the next bottleneck but to remove it, somehow.

This chapter describes our journey from treating an API gateway as a monolith to the state where developers were empowered to perform all API-related changes by themselves. In the first section, you will learn about two options of a centralized API repository and their advantages and their challenges. In the second section, you will learn how to empower developers by utilizing what you have learned throughout this book. In the third and last section, I will demonstrate how to use Azure DevOps to fully automate an Azure API Management product deployment.

© Sven Malvik 2022
S. Malvik, *Mastering Azure API Management*, https://doi.org/10.1007/978-1-4842-8011-9_9

Centralized API Repository

There exist at least two options of how to manage a centralized Git repository for APIs that are deployed to an Azure API Management instance. The first option is by using the internal Git repository of your instance while the other option uses an external Git repository such as GitHub or Azure DevOps.

Internal Repository

Before we discuss the consequences of using the internal Git repository for your APIs, let us look at how you can clone it, make changes, but also how to keep it in sync with eventual changes that are made in the Azure portal directly.

Figure 9-1 describes the steps for getting the repository's URL, username, and password. You can set the expiry date for the password to less than 30 days. To get the password, click **Generate** of the password field.

Figure 9-1. *Azure API Management Git repository*

Run `git clone <REPOSITORY_URL>` from your terminal. You will be asked for your username and password. Alternatively, run `git clone https://USERNAME:PASSWORD@<REPOSITORY_URL>` directly. In some cases, you might get an error which means that you might URL encode your password first.

The repository contains the following folders:

- **apis** contains all APIs and operations in JSON format. Furthermore, it stores descriptions that are shown in the developer portal.

- **backends** contains references and descriptions of Azure backend resources. For example, it is possible to import an Azure Function App into Azure API Management.

- **groups** contains system and custom groups with their descriptions.

- **policies** contains all policies, global, product, API, and operation in XML format.

- **portalStyles** contains the stylesheets for the developer portal.

- **portalTemplates** contains all developer portal templates. Changes in this folder will not have any effect, as discussed in the previous chapter.

- **products** contains all products as JSON files with their descriptions.

- **tags** contains tags as folders that stores JSON files with references to operations.

- **templates** contains the email templates that are sent to API consumers.

Changes that you commit and push to the repository will not take effect immediately. You need to deploy the entire repository first by clicking **Deploy to API Management**, shown in Figure 9-1.

The built-in Git repository is useful in cases where you need to make multiple changes at the same time as changing the default subscription key header for all APIs. However, as this repository does not contain everything; subscriptions, named values, etc. are missing; and neither are APIs stored in their original format, you might look at alternate options for keeping configurations and APIs under version control.

External Repository

If you work for an organization with just a few API developers that manage just a few APIs, you might consider keeping APIs, products, named values, and everything you need under version control in one centralized repository. As I mentioned in the beginning of this chapter, this worked great in my company. We treated API management as a monolith in a sense that whenever there was a change, we deployed the entire repository to our Azure API Management instances. However, this might come with a challenge. Those organizations that have not fully automated their deployments yet – like us at that time – and tend to make changes in the Azure portal directly need to reflect those changes in the repository as well, something which is not always done.

When our Azure API Management developer left the company and we had to add a new operation (endpoint) to an existing API, we knew that we had to deploy the entire repository. The challenge was that the repository was not in sync with what was deployed. There were many minor differences that we did not understand. What we later realized was that some changes were just not deployed yet, while other changes were forgotten to be reflected in the codebase of the repository and vice versa. For us, deploying the entire codebase was a great risk.

Figure 9-2 shows the workflow of an API deployment using a central API repository. As APIs are deployed from a central API repository to Azure API Management, it is neseccary to ensure integrity through automation. Both, an application repository and the central API repository, must have the same API changes. Otherwise, you might, in a failure situation, debug a web service that behaves differently from what is deployed.

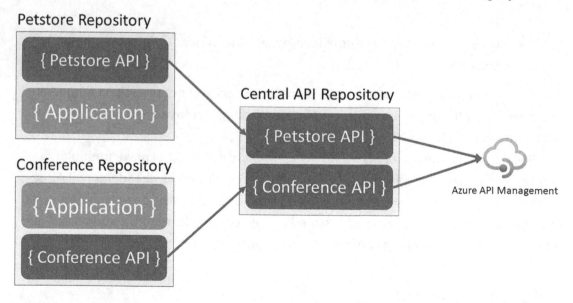

Figure 9-2. *API deploying workflow with centralized API repository*

As we were growing, more API developers changed the codebase which led to more deployments and more risk. Furthermore, we used Azure Resource Management (ARM) templates to deploy our APIs and products because it is the native platform for infrastructure as code in Azure. The challenge with ARM templates is that it is harder to master, especially for developers that work most of their working hours with languages such as Java, C#, or Go and that use ARM templates only for a couple of hours a month. We will look at API deployments with ARM in a later chapter.

A centralized API repository works great for small development units where you can gain experience with Azure API Management. For larger organizations with many API developers, I learned that even if you maintain one Azure API Management instance in each environment only, it is the API developers who should be responsible for the entire API lifecycle. As you have learned throughout this book, it is possible to deploy APIs, products, and named values individually, so there is no reason to introduce a bottleneck other than access restrictions. You will learn how to secure your Azure API Management instance in a later chapter.

Application Repositories

In the previous section, we discussed two approaches of using centralized Git repositories for your APIs. In this section, we will discuss a decentralized approach where your APIs are kept close to the web services. Instead of copying an API from the application repository to the central API repository before it gets deployed to Azure API Management, this approach lets you deploy an API directly from the application repository to Azure API Management, as Figure 9-3 shows.

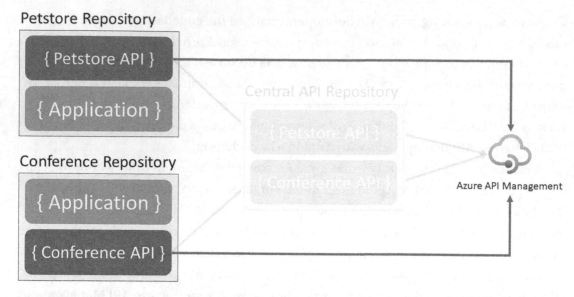

Figure 9-3. *APIs are deployed from the application repository*

Deploying directly from the application repository gives development teams strong ownership of the entire deployment workflow. Instead of doing a hand-over to the team that administrates the central API repository, the development teams themselves can deploy and thus be responsible.

When my company moved from a central API repository to a setup where the development teams got full ownership of the API lifecycles, we immediately removed a bottleneck. Development teams could deploy their APIs when they were ready, and they did not need to wait for the administration team anymore, which was a huge relief for all of us.

However, this approach where development teams can use their own CI/CD pipelines to deploy APIs to Azure API Management might require some preparation. Not every single team in the same organization should create its own API deployment process. Having ten development teams might result in ten different solutions, or ten times the same solutions; both are bad, as they require more developers to implement the same. You might also end up in a situation where developers create for your standard's unsecure deployment workflows. Instead, a platform team might want to create tooling that is easy to use for the developers. You have already learned throughout this book how to deploy APIs. You can do the same for products and named values and create easy to use pipelines or tools.

Product Deployment with Azure Pipeline

In this chapter, we talked about ownership and how to theoretically deploy an API by creating easy-to-use tooling for the developers. While API ownership can often be mapped to individual teams, products might include APIs that are owned by several teams, thus there is no clear ownership of a product. This should be avoided if possible. However, as this might be a challenge, it is even more important to have an automated deployment workflow in place. In this section, I will therefore show you how to create a CI/CD workflow for a product with Azure pipeline with YAML syntax in Azure DevOps.

Listing 9-1 shows a JSON file that describes a single Azure API Management product and its APIs. I named the product "Demo Services," and it contains two APIs, `petstore-api` and `conference-api`, that you remember from previous chapters.

Listing 9-1. Single product configuration (demo_services.json)

```
{
    "Demo-Services": {
        "id": "demo-services",
        "title": "Demo Services",
        "description": "Demo product",
        "apis": [
            "petstore-api",
            "conference-api"
        ]
    }
}
```

To deploy this product and to add those two APIs, I will use the PowerShell cmdlets that you have seen in Chapter 3 - APIs and Products, so we will not discuss the deployment process itself, but instead focus on the Azure pipeline with YAML syntax.

Listing 9-2 shows a specific product–Demo Services–pipeline with YAML syntax that uses a template that is responsible for deploying any product. This template resides in a different repository (`mycompany/apim-tools`) that a platform team might own, so all development teams can use this template. Development teams need "simply" pass all required parameters such as the product configuration file and the product id to this template. You will find detailed information about Azure pipelines with YAML syntax in Microsoft Azure's documentation.

Listing 9-2. Azure pipeline for Azure API Management product deployment

```
trigger:
- main

pool:
  vmImage: 'windows-2019'

name: $(Build.SourceBranchName)-$(Date:yyyyMMdd)-$(Build.BuildId)

resources:
  repositories:
    - repository: apim-tools
      type: git
      name: mycompany/apim-tools
      ref: refs/heads/master

variables:
  productId: demo-services

steps:
- checkout: self
- checkout: apim-tools
- template: apim-product-template.yaml@apim-tools
  parameters:
    ENVIRONMENT: 'test'
    APIM_SERVICE_CONNECTION: test-sc
    PRODUCT_CONFIGPATH: .\demo-services.json
    PRODUCT_ID: '$(productId)'
    APIM_TOOLS_ARTIFACTNAME: apim-tools
```

Listing 9-3 shows the product deployment template. It requires five parameters:

- ENVIRONMENT references the Azure API Management instance. In case you have several instances per environment, this needs to be more specific.

- APIM_SERVICE_CONNECTION defines the name of a service connection in Azure DevOps. You will find detailed information about service connections in Azure DevOps on Microsoft Azure's documentation.

- PRODUCT_ID specifies the product within the product configuration file. You might want to define more than one.

- PRODUCT_CONFIGPATH defines the path of the product configuration file.

- APIM_TOOLS_ARTIFACTNAME defines the name of the repository name that is defined in Listing 9-2.

The template contains one step that executes a PowerShell script and passes the required parameters.

Listing 9-3. Product deployment template (apim-product-template.yaml)

```
parameters:
- name: ENVIRONMENT
  type: string
- name: APIM_SERVICE_CONNECTION
  type: string
- name: PRODUCT_ID
  type: string
- name: PRODUCT_CONFIGPATH
  type: string
- name: APIM_TOOLS_ARTIFACTNAME
  type: string

steps:
- task: AzurePowerShell@5
  displayName: 'Deploy ${{ parameters.PRODUCT_ID }} product'
  inputs:
    azureSubscription: ${{ parameters.APIM_SERVICE_CONNECTION }}
    scriptType: 'FilePath'
    ScriptPath: ./${{ parameters.APIM_TOOLS_ARTIFACTNAME }}/apim-scripts/
    APIM_Product.ps1
    ScriptArguments: '-Environment "${{ parameters.ENVIRONMENT }}"
    -ProductConfigPath ${{ parameters.PRODUCT_CONFIGPATH }} -ProductId "${{
    parameters.PRODUCT_ID }}"'
    preferredAzurePowerShellVersion: 3.5.0
```

This example shall give you an idea of how you might want to set up a code-based workflow that deploys to Azure API Management.

Summary

I hope this chapter helped you to understand the pros and cons of having a centralized API repository and what options Azure API Management provides you. However, storing APIs and products in repositories is one part of the equation. The other part is how to deploy them. I gave you an example of a product deployment that you can adapt for API deployments as well by referencing a script `APIM_API.ps1` – that you will implement – instead of a script for product deployments `APIM_Product.ps1`, as in this example. We used Azure Pipelines for this as this is YAML code which can live side-by-side with your application in the same repository.

CHAPTER 10

Developing Policies

Policies are the heart of Azure API Management, where you change the behavior of APIs such as transforming backend responses from XML to JSON, routing traffic to new backend web services, or validating headers. As developing policies in XML and C# is not a trivial task – combining two languages in the same file is hard – it is even more important to use tools that support you.

This chapter teaches you to be most effective in developing policies in Azure API Management. You know already where to implement policies in the Azure portal. However, there are a few utilities that I have not mentioned yet and that you learn about in the first section. In the second section, you will use *Visual Studio Code* and install an Azure API Management extension which improves your productivity and development experience compared to the Azure portal. In the last section, I will show how you can test policies with the *Pester* testing framework for PowerShell.

Azure Portal

Developing policies in the Azure portal is a good way to try out ideas, but a dangerous way to do serious coding with. Changes that you apply from the Azure portal in an Azure API Management instance are not in any codebase, nor are they under version control unless you apply them manually. However, the Azure portal provides ready-to-use code snippets that can help you to get started quickly.

Figure 10-1 shows how to get started with ready-to-use policies in the Azure portal. Navigate to an API, a product, or the global policy as shown in the figure and click **Add policy**.

© Sven Malvik 2022
S. Malvik, *Mastering Azure API Management*, https://doi.org/10.1007/978-1-4842-8011-9_10

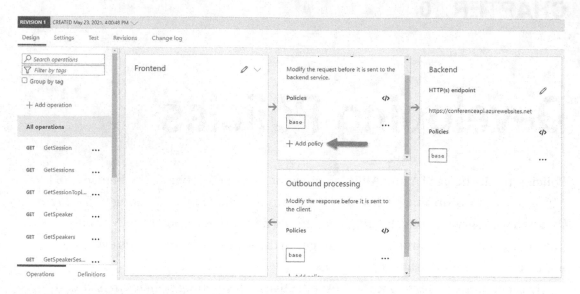

Figure 10-1. *Adding ready-to-use policies*

You see a list of inbound policies that you can choose from as Figure 10-2 shows. When you click on one of them, you can configure it. For example, when you click on **Limit call rate**, you can configure this policy by setting the numbers of calls, renewal period, counter key, and an increment condition. Whatever ready-to-use policy you choose, you can configure it by filling setting values in the configuration form.

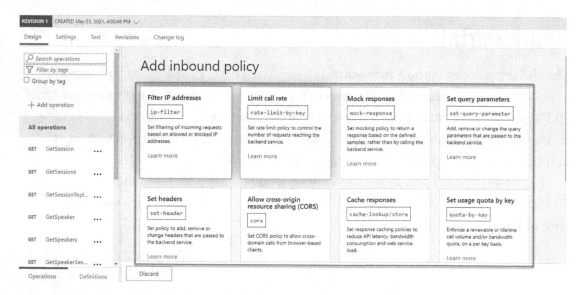

Figure 10-2. *List of ready-to-use policies*

Figure 10-3 shows the configuration form of the **Set query parameter** policy where you can set the name, value, and action of one or many query parameters.

Inbound processing

Modify the request before it is sent to the backend service.

Set query parameters

Add, remove or change the query parameters that are passed to the backend service.

Learn more about "set-query-parameter" policy.

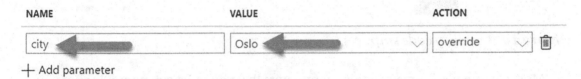

NAME	VALUE	ACTION
city	Oslo	override

+ Add parameter

Figure 10-3. *Setting query parameters*

What happens after you saved the new policy configuration is that it is added to the inbound section of the policy. Instead of coding a policy yourself, you used predefined code snippets that you can change further directly within the policy editor as the following code demonstrates:

```
<inbound>
    <base />
    <set-query-parameter name="city" exists-action="override">
        <value>Oslo</value>
    </set-query-parameter>
</inbound>
```

Another way where you can use predefined code snippets is when you click **Show snippets** from within the policy editor, as shown in Figure 10-4. The list of policies to choose from is larger than what you have seen before. When you click on a snippet, the code for it will be inserted where you have positioned the curser. That means that you can add code snippets in all four policy sections, </inbound>, </backend>, </outbound>, and </on-error>.

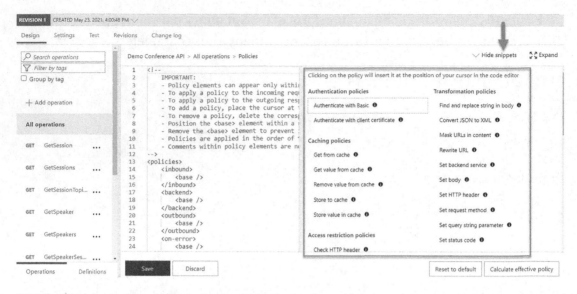

Figure 10-4.   *Policy code snippets*

Most of the code snippets require parameters that you must set manually after you have selected and inserted a code snippet.

The policy editor might be a good choice for trying out policy changes without setting up a development environment first. I use it sometimes for exactly that, making quick changes that I do not want to have under version control yet.

Visual Studio Code Extension

When it comes to APIs and policies that are under development and that I have under version control, I use Visual Studio Code (VS Code); it is free of charge and available for all major operating systems. It comes with a marketplace where you can choose from hundreds of extensions such as those for Azure and API Management. Download and install VS Code by following the documentation.

Installation

Select the extensions icon on the left-hand side or navigate to "View/Extensions" from the top menu as Figure 10-5 shows. Type "Azure API Management" in the extensions search field to find the extension and click on it. On the right-hand side, you find an **Install** button; click on it.

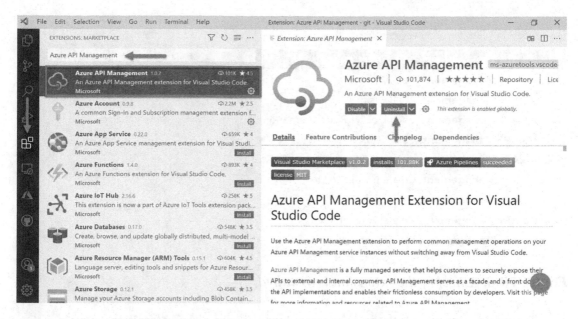

Figure 10-5. *Install Azure API Management extension for VS Code*

Before we can use the Azure API Management, we need some additional extensions that are required. Search for the following extensions in the same way as you did for the Azure API Management extension and install them:

- Azure Account to sign in to your account and filter your subscriptions.

- C# for syntax highlighting and IntelliSense.

- REST Client for sending test requests.

Congratulations, the installation was successful. To get an overview of all available commands that this extension provides, open the command palette and search for "Azure API Management." Click **Ctrl+Shift+P** if you use a Windows computer and **Cmd-Shift+P** if you are using a Mac computer. Figure 10-6 shows how the command palette looks like. As the name suggests, it accepts all kinds of commands. Many of them have a prefix followed by a colon that indicates the extension it belongs to.

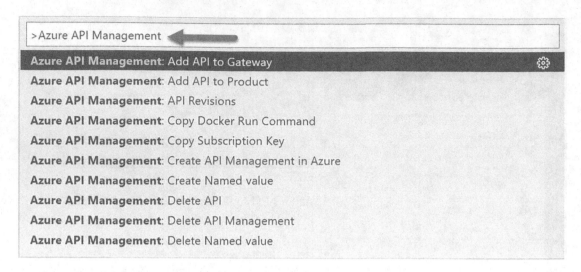

Figure 10-6. *Check if the extension is installed*

Most of the commands that you see in Figure 10-6 are already familiar to you as PowerShell cmdlets. This extension provides a simpler way to work with Azure API Management without first setting the context of your instance and then writing PowerShell cmdlets. This is especially helpful when developing policies.

You installed another extension, *Azure Account*. You need this extension to sign in to your Azure account. Search for *Azure Sign In* and click on it, as Figure 10-7 demonstrates. Follow the instructions to sign in to your account with your running instance of Azure API Management.

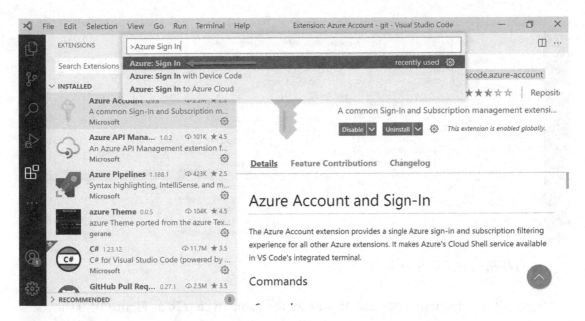

Figure 10-7. *Sign in to your Azure account*

Now that you are signed in to your Azure account, you can use extensions such as the Azure API Management extension.

Developing a Policy

Developing policies with the Azure API Management extension for VS Code helps API developers to be more productive as it provides IntelliSense features such as code completion for policy expressions.

The following example demonstrates a policy that sets a correlation ID to each request. We will use this example to demonstrate the debugger of this extension.

Select Azure in the left-hand menu as Figure 10-8 demonstrates. You need to be signed in in order to proceed. After a few seconds, all subscriptions that are connected to your account appear and list your Azure API Management instances. In my case, I selected my *Visual Studio Enterprise Subscription* which has one instance with the name *mastering-apim*. Open the *global policy*. In the inbound section, start then typing `set-` without the leading < character that you would usually use in XML code. A sorted list of policy expressions appears. Select `set-variable` to insert the complete policy expression.

Figure 10-8. *IntelliSense for policies*

Repeat the same with `set-header` and set the value to `corrId` as Figure 10-9 shows. The figure also shows four arrows which mark the next cursor positions when typing **tab**. When you are on an attribute where only certain values are valid like in case of `exists-action`, a list with valid attribute values appears.

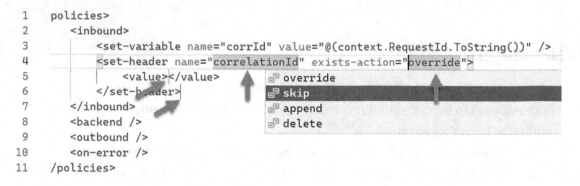

Figure 10-9. *Editing a policy in VS Code*

Listing 10-1 shows the complete code for this example. It adds the identifier of a request generated by Azure API Management to each request as the header `correlationId`. There are other options to create a correlation ID that might fit your use case better.

Listing 10-1. Policy for adding a simple correlation ID to the request

```
<policies>
    <inbound>
        <set-variable name="corrId" value="@(context.RequestId.
        ToString())" />
        <set-header name="correlationId" exists-action="skip">
            <value>@(context.Variables.GetValueOrDefault<string>("corr
            Id"))</value>
        </set-header>
    </inbound>
    <backend />
    <outbound />
<on-error />
</policies>
```

The preceding example could be simplified by setting @(context.RequestId.
ToString()) of corrId directly as the value of the header. However, we will later modify
corrId, so let us stick to it for now.

Testing an API

In this section, you will test a policy by using the **Test Operation** feature of this
extension. As we know from other languages such as Java and C#, the possibility to easily
test our code is an elementary part in software development. The extension for Azure
API Management provides partly this possibility. Partly because this feature does not
automatically validate the response as we know from unit tests. Testing in the context of
this extension means sending a request to an API operation.

Figure 10-10 shows how to create a request for testing an API operation. Select
one operation such as *GetTopics* and right-click on it. Click **Test Operation** to create a
request.

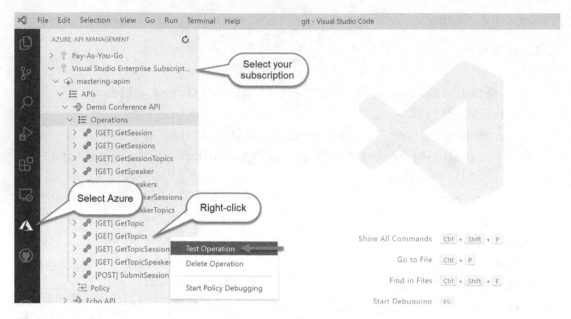

Figure 10-10. *Create a request in VS Code*

In the editor on the right-hand side in VS Code appears the configuration for a request, as shown in Figure 10-9. The configuration describes the request method GET, the endpoint URL `https://mastering-apim.azure-api.net/conf/topics`, and two headers. Take notice of the subscription-key header as you might have changed it previously to *ApiKey*. You must now replace `{{azure-api-management-subscription-key}}` with your actual key. When you have done this, click **Send Request,** as shown in Figure 10-11.

```
     Send Request
1    GET https://mastering-apim.azure-api.net/conf/topics HTTP/1.1
2    Ocp-Apim-Subscription-Key: {{azure-api-management-subscription-key}}
3    Ocp-Apim-Trace: true
4
5
```

Figure 10-11. *Sending a request from VS Code*

A second tab in the VS Code editor appears in a split window with the response of your request showing the HTTP status, date, and headers, as Figure 10-12 shows. The `Ocp-Apim-Trace-Location` header points to a Json file which contains details you might need to trace a request and response in case of an error.

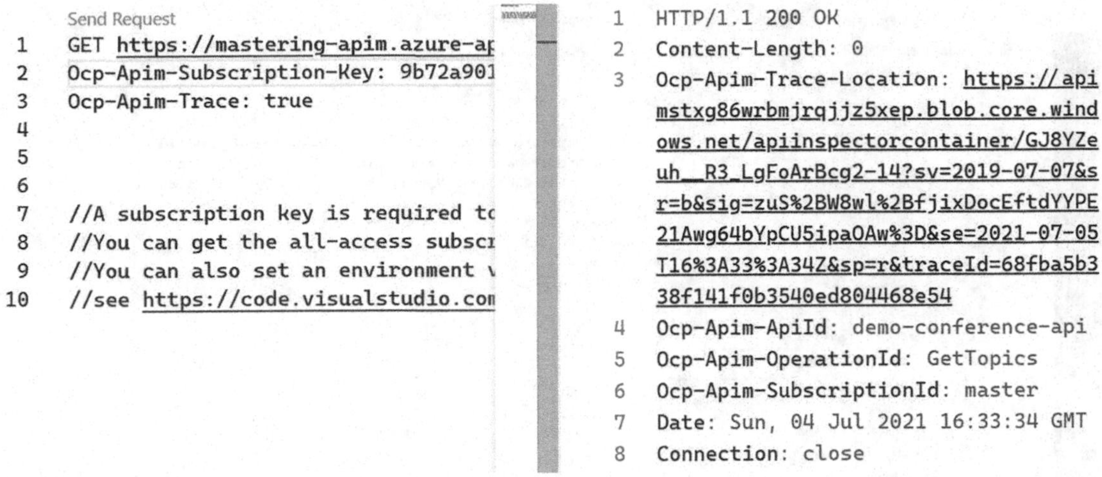

```
    Send Request                                  1   HTTP/1.1 200 OK
 1  GET https://mastering-apim.azure-ap           2   Content-Length: 0
 2  Ocp-Apim-Subscription-Key: 9b72a901           3   Ocp-Apim-Trace-Location: https://api
 3  Ocp-Apim-Trace: true                              mstxg86wrbmjrqjjz5xep.blob.core.wind
 4                                                     ows.net/apiinspectorcontainer/GJ8YZe
 5                                                     uh__R3_LgFoArBcg2-14?sv=2019-07-07&s
 6                                                     r=b&sig=zuS%2BW8wl%2BfjixDocEftdYYPE
 7  //A subscription key is required to               21Awg64bYpCU5ipaOAw%3D&se=2021-07-05
 8  //You can get the all-access subscr               T16%3A33%3A34Z&sp=r&traceId=68fba5b3
 9  //You can also set an environment v               38f141f0b3540ed804468e54
10  //see https://code.visualstudio.com          4   Ocp-Apim-ApiId: demo-conference-api
                                                  5   Ocp-Apim-OperationId: GetTopics
                                                  6   Ocp-Apim-SubscriptionId: master
                                                  7   Date: Sun, 04 Jul 2021 16:33:34 GMT
                                                  8   Connection: close
```

Figure 10-12. *Response in VS Code*

Sending requests with this extension might be a convenient way for many to develop and test their API policies from the same IDE. However, API developers often use tools such as Postman to create and collect requests that they use to develop APIs. For those developers, it might be easier to stick to these existing request collections instead of creating new requests in VS Code.

Debugging a Policy

You will now create a debugging session that connects to your remote Azure API Management gateway. **Right-click** on the API operation that you want to debug. In my case, I stick to GetTopics. As Figure 10-13 shows, you start a debugging session by selecting **Start Policy Debugging**.

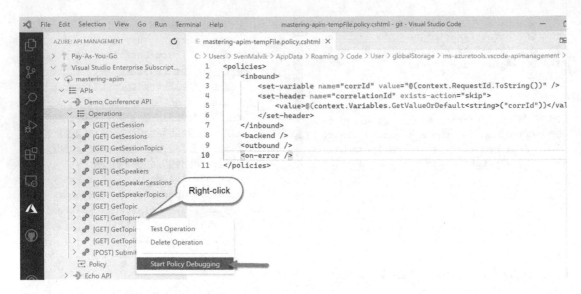

Figure 10-13. *Starting a policy debugging session*

A new tab for the request appears as you have seen when you tested an API operation. Click **Send Request** to send a call. A new tab appears that looks like the one shown in Figure 10-14. The debugger stops at the first policy expression of the effective policy.

Remember   The effective policy includes policies from all scopes.

In this example, the curser has first stopped at line 3 of the global policy as it is the first policy expression of the effective policy. Click the **Step Over** icon to get to the second policy expression. On the left-hand side of the editor, you see a list of available variables, context and corrId.

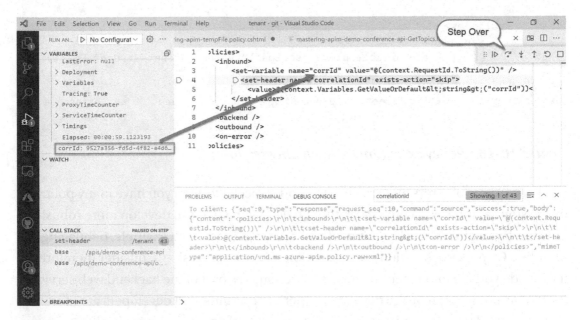

Figure 10-14. *Debugging a policy*

You have learned to step through an effective policy by using a simple example with two policy expressions. Imagine a policy where you define expressions in different policies and at different scopes. Finding an error becomes very hard as the following example will demonstrate.

Listing 10-2 defines a policy expression for setting the users email address in a variable userEmail.

Listing 10-2. Policy expression in the GetTopics API operation

```
<inbound>
    <set-variable name="userEmail" value="@(context.User.Email)" />
    <base />
</inbound>
```

What happens when we initiate a debugging session and send a request without signing in first is getting an error, as Figure 10-15 shows. The user does not exist, thus the object reference for *User* is *null*.

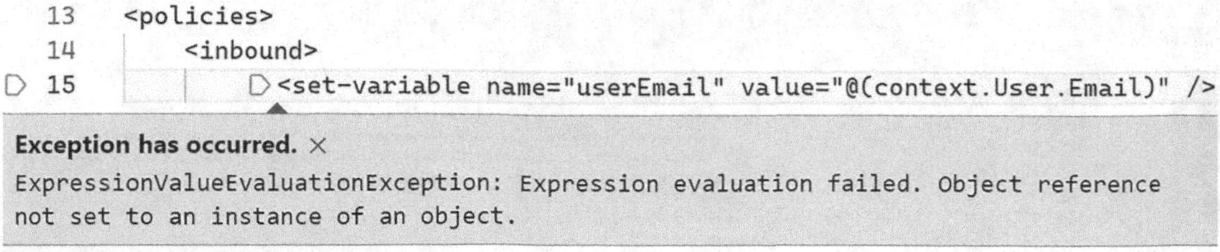

```
13    <policies>
14        <inbound>
15            <set-variable name="userEmail" value="@(context.User.Email)" />
```

Exception has occurred. ✕

ExpressionValueEvaluationException: Expression evaluation failed. Object reference
not set to an instance of an object.

Figure 10-15. *Policy exception in debugging session*

Those kinds of errors might be hard to find, especially when you have many policy
expressions at multiple scopes. Even though debugging helps to develop more robust
policies, try to minimize the amount of policy expressions. As an example, debugging
multiline C# policy expressions is not possible with this extension. Consider therefore
if the code you are implementing makes more sense as part of the backend web service
itself. This might improve the developer experience as most API developers are more
familiar with the tools they use when developing a backend web service itself.

Summary

In this chapter, you learned two ways of developing policies in Azure API Management.
First, you used the policy editor within the Azure portal for API Management where you
can insert policy expressions by using policy snippets. This built-in editor is a great way
to make quick changes when you only have your browser available. The second way of
developing policies is by using the Azure API Management extension for VS Code. This
extension has IntelliSense features such as code completion that help to create policies
faster than relying on documentation only. It also helps to build more robust policies as
we can start debugging sessions and follow a request through an effective policy.

## CHAPTER 11

Deploying APIs

APIs can be deployed in many ways, with the Azure CLI, PowerShell, ARM templates, Azure Bicep, Terraform, and many other tools and technologies that are available. When I started working in a project that involved Azure API Management, the APIs and their policies were deployed with ARM templates. Deploying Azure resources with ARM is a common way to manage resources in Azure and to deploy infrastructure. This does not mean that ARM templates are a great fit when it comes to deploying APIs to Azure API Management. I think the opposite is the case and the Azure CLI and PowerShell are better suited where developers are involved.

This chapter will discuss several options of deploying APIs and policies to Azure API Management and then discuss the pros and cons of each of them, so you can decide for yourself what is the best option for you and your technology eco system.

ARM Templates

Infrastructure as code is a common practice to automate deployments. Azure provides the Azure Resource Manager templates (ARM templates), where you define infrastructure as JSON-like files. Those engineers that define and deploy infrastructure and services such as networking, storage, or Azure API Management are often not the same as those that develop the web services and the APIs.

ARM templates are not limited to networking and services; you can also use them to deploy APIs, products, and policies to Azure API Management. The deployment includes three files:

- The **ARM template** *demo-conference.json* describes what Azure API Management instance to deploy to and the location of the API and policy files.

- The **API** *demo-conference-api.json* is a simplified OpenAPI specification of the Demo Conference API with only one operation.

- The **API policy** *demo-conference-api.policy.json* sets an outbound header.

Figure 11-1 illustrates how to deploy the Demo Conference API and its API policy. In this example, I keep the ARM template on my local machine for demonstration purposes. However, this is not a requirement; you can store your ARM template together with your other files at a downloadable location such as an Azure Storage Account. When referencing files such as the API and policy, the value of the URIs can't be local files. The Azure Resource Manager must be able to access them. You must therefore provide a URI value where the files are downloadable as HTTP or HTTPS.

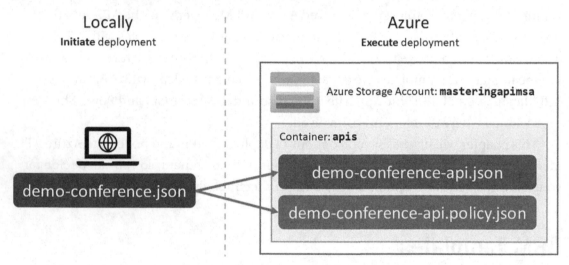

Figure 11-1. *API deployment with ARM*

Listing 11-1 shows a simplified version of the Demo Conference API that I downloaded to my local machine and named `demo-conference.json`. The API describes one operation, *GetTopics*. You can use the full version of this API that is available at `http://conferenceapi.azurewebsites.net/?format=json`.

Listing 11-1. Simplified Demo Conference API

```
{
    "swagger": "2.0",
    "info": {
        "title": "Demo Conference API",
        "description": "Demo API",
```

```
    "version": "2.0.0"
},
"host": "conferenceapi.azurewebsites.net",
"schemes": [
    "http",
    "https"
],
"securityDefinitions": {
    "apiKeyHeader": {
        "type": "apiKey",
        "name": "Ocp-Apim-Subscription-Key",
        "in": "header"
    },
    "apiKeyQuery": {
        "type": "apiKey",
        "name": "subscription-key",
        "in": "query"
    }
},
"security": [
    {
        "apiKeyHeader": []
    },
    {
        "apiKeyQuery": []
    }
],
"paths": {
    "/topics": {
        "get": {
            "operationId": "GetTopics",
            "responses": {
                "200": {
                    "description": "OK"
                }
```

```
            },
            "produces": [
                "application/vnd.collection+json"
            ]
        }
    }
  }
}
```

Listing 11-2 describes the API policy that I also have on my local machine. It sets one outbound header.

Listing 11-2. Demo Conference API policy

```
<policies>
    <inbound>
        <base />
    </inbound>
    <backend>
        <base />
    </backend>
    <outbound>
        <set-header name="X-myHeader" exists-action="override">
            <value>My header</value>
        </set-header>
        <base />
    </outbound>
    <on-error>
        <base />
    </on-error>
</policies>
```

I have two files, the API specification itself and the API policy, both are on my local machine. In order to be available to the Azure Resource Manager, both files must be downloadable which is not the case now.

As illustrated in Figure 11-1, we need an Azure Storage Account masteringapimsa and a container where we can store both files. Listing 11-3 describes how to create an

Azure Storage Account with PowerShell. Set first the context and define the subscription you are using. To create a new Azure Storage Account, use the Azure PowerShell cmdlet `New-AzStorageAccount`.For the purpose of this demonstration, I set `SkuName` to the cheapest option *LRS* (Local Redundancy Storage).

Listing 11-3. Creating Azure Storage Account

```
# Set the correct context
$context = Get-AzSubscription -SubscriptionId "b0e68700-2b10-4f92-858a-36d2
a98748b8"
Set-AzContext $context

# Create storage account
$storageAccount = New-AzStorageAccount `
    -ResourceGroupName "mastering-apim-rg" `
    -Name "masteringapimsa" `
    -Location "West Europe" `
    -SkuName "Standard_LRS"
```

We store our files in a container of our Azure Storage Account. I name the container `apis`. By default, the container and any blobs in it can be accessed only by the owner of the storage account. To provide full read access to anonymous users, we set the permission to `Container`. In a production environment, you would delegate access to containers with shared access signatures (SAS). To focus on deploying an API and its policy with ARM, I create a container with full read access as Listing 11-4 shows.

Listing 11-4. Creating container in Azure Storage Account

```
# Create a container
New-AzStorageContainer -Name "apis" -Context $storageAccount.Context -Permission
Container
```

Upload both files, `demo-conference-api.json` and `demo-conference-api.policy.xml` into the container `apis`. Both files should be publicly available via `https://masteringapimsa.blob.core.windows.net/arm/demo-conference-api.json` and `https://masteringapimsa.blob.core.windows.net/arm/demo-conference-api.policy.xml`.

What is missing is the ARM template that describes to the Azure Resource Manager what to deploy. Listing 11-5 shows the ARM template for deploying our Demo Conference API and its policy. Our ARM template has four sections:

- In **parameters**, we define the name of the Azure API Management instance and the location of the Azure Storage Account.

- In **variables**, we define the API name that is used twice later in the ARM template and the resource location within the storage account.

- In **resources**, we define the resources that we are deploying, the API and its policy.

- In **outputs**, we do not define anything as we do not have following steps that would require input from this deployment.

I want to highlight the two resources of this ARM template. They define both a type, name, and two properties. For APIs, the **type** is `Microsoft.ApiManagement/service/apis`; for API policies `Microsoft.ApiManagement/service/apis/policies`. We can concatenate the resource **name** of both resources with `apiName` and `resourceLocation` variable. The policy resource gets `policy` at the end of the name. The **properties** for the API and its policy have a `contentFormat` that I set to `swagger-link-json` for the API and `xml-link` for the policy. The `contentValue` of both properties is the downloadable URL of the API and the policy that are stored in the storage account.

Listing 11-5. ARM template

```
{
    "$schema": "https://schema.management.azure.com/schemas/2019-04-01/
    deploymentTemplate.json#",
    "contentVersion": "1.0.0.0",
    "parameters": {
      "apiManagementServiceName": {
        "type": "string",
        "defaultValue": "mastering-apim"
      },
      "_artifactsLocation": {
        "type": "string",
        "defaultValue": "https://masteringapimsa.blob.core.windows.net"
```

```
    }
  },
  "variables": {
    "apiName": "demo-conference-api",
    "resourceLocation":  "[concat(parameters('_artifactsLocation'), '/
    apis/')]"
  },
  "resources": [
    {
      "apiVersion": "2018-01-01",
      "type": "Microsoft.ApiManagement/service/apis",
      "name": "[concat(parameters('apiManagementServiceName'), '/',
      variables('apiName'))]",
      "properties": {
        "contentFormat": "swagger-link-json",
        "contentValue": "[concat(variables('resourceLocation'),
        variables('apiName'), '.json')]",
        "path": "conf"
      }
    },
    {
      "apiVersion": "2018-01-01",
      "type": "Microsoft.ApiManagement/service/apis/policies",
      "name": "[concat(parameters('apiManagementServiceName'), '/',
      variables('apiName'), '/', 'policy')]",
      "dependsOn": [
        "[concat('Microsoft.ApiManagement/service/', parameters('apiManag
        ementServiceName'), '/apis/', variables('apiName'))]"
      ],
      "properties": {
        "contentFormat": "xml-link",
        "policyContent": "[concat(variables('resourceLocation'),
        variables('apiName'), '.policy.xml')]"
      }
    }
```

```
    ],
    "outputs": {
    }
  }
}
```

You can keep the ARM template locally or store it side-by-side with your API and policy. To deploy both resources with ARM, I use the Azure CLI command `az deployment group create`, as shown in Listing 11-6. The command requires two parameters, the resource group `--resource-group` and the ARM template `--template-file`. You can provide an URI for the ARM template instead of the local file with `--template-uri`.

Listing 11-6. Deploying an ARM template with Azure CLI

```
az deployment group create `
    --resource-group mastering-apim-rg `
    --template-file demo-conference.json
```

If you are not familiar with ARM templates, do not worry, there are other options for deploying APIs and policies to Azure API Management. In fact, many developers of web services that deploy APIs and policies occasionally find it hard to work with ARM templates. If you are a developer that focuses primarily on writing application code, you should consider either creating a tool that can generate ARM templates or choosing one of the other deployment options. The reason for that is that ARM templates are often hard to implement for developers as Azure is not their primary domain.

Bicep

Azure Bicep is a new domain specific language (DSL) and is developed by Microsoft. It aims to simplify the authoring experience with a cleaner syntax, improved type safety, and better support for modularity and code reuse. Azure Bicep is a transparent abstraction over ARM and ARM templates, which means anything that can be done in an ARM template can be done in Bicep.

If you have already an ARM template, you can convert it to Bicep code with the Azure CLI command `az bicep decompile`, as Listing 11-7 shows.

Listing 11-7. Convert an ARM template to Bicep

```
az bicep decompile --file demo-conference.json
```

The output of this command is a Bicep file `demo-conference.bicep`, as Listing 11-8 shows.

Listing 11-8. Bicep code of an API deployment

```
param apiManagementServiceName string = 'mastering-apim'
param artifactsLocation string = 'https://masteringapimsa.blob.core.
windows.net'

var apiName = 'demo-conference-api'
var resourceLocation = '${artifactsLocation}/arm/'

resource apiManagementServiceName_apiName 'Microsoft.ApiManagement/service/
apis@2018-01-01' = {
  name: '${apiManagementServiceName}/${apiName}'
  properties: {
    contentFormat: 'swagger-link-json'
    contentValue: '${resourceLocation}${apiName}.json'
    path: 'conf'
  }
}

resource apiManagementServiceName_apiName_policy 'Microsoft.ApiManagement/
service/apis/policies@2018-01-01' = {
  parent: apiManagementServiceName_apiName
  name: 'policy'
  properties: {
    contentFormat: 'xml-link'
    policyContent: '${resourceLocation}${apiName}.policy.xml'
  }
}
```

The Bicep code describes the same as the equivalent ARM template. Compared to the ARM template with 44 lines of code, the Bicep code has only 23 lines of code, a reduction by almost 50%.

To deploy the Bicep file, you execute the same command as you did with the ARM template; this time with the `demo-conference.bicep` file.

```
az deployment group create `
    --resource-group mastering-apim-rg `
    --template-file demo-conference.bicep
```

What happens when you deploy a Bicep file is that it gets compiled to an ARM template and uses this as an intermediate format to deploy Azure resources. It means that if you already have an ARM template, you do not need to decompile it to a Bicep file. However, from the perspective of a developer, Bicep files are better readable and therefore easier to maintain. If you are starting out with Azure deployments, I recommend starting with Bicep over ARM templates. This is where Microsoft has its focus and is the de facto standard going forward. You get more information about Azure Bicep in the official documentation.

REST

Another option for deploying Azure resources is by using the Azure REST API. It provides a very flexible way of managing resources in Azure as it can be used almost anywhere, high-level languages such as Java and C#, PowerShell, or tools like Postman and cURL. However, using REST might add some additional complexity as you as a developer need to manage dependencies between Azure resources yourself, something that ARM and Bicep can manage for you.

This section demonstrates how to use cURL to deploy the Demo Conference API and its policy. Listing 11-9 shows four variables:

- **SERVICE** defines the name of the Azure API Management instance.

- **RESOURCE_GROUP** and **SUBSCRIPTION_ID** define what the name suggests for the service.

- **URL** defines the Azure REST endpoint for deploying an API.

Listing 11-9. Defining variables for a REST API call

```
SERVICE="mastering-apim"
RESOURCE_GROUP="mastering-apim-rg"
```

```
SUBSCRIPTION_ID="b0e68700-2b10-4f92-858a-36d2a98748b8"
URL=https://mastering-apim.management.azure-api.net/
subscriptions/$SUBSCRIPTION_ID/resourceGroups/$RESOURCE_GROUP/providers/
Microsoft.ApiManagement/service/$SERVICE
```

To access the endpoint URL, a user needs a valid shared access signature (SAS) token. One way of getting a SAS token is by navigating to your Azure API Management instance in the Azure portal and selecting the **Management API** pane from the left-hand menu, as shown in Figure 11-2. Scroll down to *Access token* and click **Generate**. By default, the SAS token is valid for 30 days.

Figure 11-2. *Copy Shared Access Signature (SAS) token*

Copy the SAS token and set the value as shown in the following; we need to construct the cURL command:

```
SAS="YOUR_SAS_TOKEN"
```

The cURL command that we create expects values of the API that we set as JSON payload. Listing 11-10 shows a minimal request payload for deploying an API.

- The value of **id** is the reference to this API resource.

- The value of **type** is the same for all API deployments.

- I set the **name** of this API to demo-conference-api.

- In **properties**, we set an array with required parameters such as the URL to our API, format, and the path. I added some more attributes to be consistent with the previous examples in this chapter.

Listing 11-10. Request payload for deploying an API

```
{
    "id": "/subscriptions/$sid/resourceGroups/$rg/providers/Microsoft.
    ApiManagement/service/$service/apis/demo-conference-api",
    "type": "Microsoft.ApiManagement/service/apis",
    "name": "demo-conference-api",
    "properties": {
      "displayName": "Demo Conference API",
      "value": "http://conferenceapi.azurewebsites.net/?format=json",
      "format": "swagger-link-json",
      "description": "This is the Demo Conference API",
      "subscriptionRequired": true,
      "path": "conf"
    }
}
```

Store the JSON payload in a file *./api-data.json* and execute the cURL command with the HTTP request method **PUT** and the payload `--data @api-data.json`, as shown in Listing 11-11. This will deploy the API to your Azure API Management instance.

Listing 11-11. Deploying API with cURL

```
curl -X PUT -H "Authorization: $SAS" -H "Content-Type: application/json"
--data @api-data.json $URL/apis/demo-conference-api?api-version=2019-12-01
```

To request the deployed API, run the same command with the HTTP method **GET** and without the payload, as shown in the following:

```
curl -X GET -H "Authorization: $sas" -H "Content-Type: application/json"
$url/apis/demo-conference-api?api-version=2019-12-01
```

To deploy a policy with the Azure REST API, you have two options; you can either host the policy on an HTTP endpoint accessible from the API Management service or you can define the policy as payload as shown in Listing 11-12. I store the payload in a file *./apipolicy-data.json* that defines a `properties` object with two members, `format` and `value`. As I want to define the policy as payload, the format is `xml` and the value the policy itself.

Listing 11-12. Simple API policy

```
{
    "properties": {
      "format": "xml",
      "value": "<policies>
      <inbound>
          <base />
      </inbound>
      <backend>
          <base />
      </backend>
      <outbound>
          <set-header name=\"X-myHeader\" exists-action=\"override\">
              <value>My header</value>
          </set-header>
          <base />
      </outbound>
      <on-error>
          <base />
      </on-error>
  </policies>
  "
    }
}
```

Execute the cURL command shown in Listing 11-13 for deploying the API policy.

Listing 11-13. Deploying API policy with Azure REST API

```
curl -X PUT -H "Authorization: $sas" -H "Content-Type: application/
json" --data @apipolicy-data.json $url/apis/demo-conference-api/policies/
policy?api-version=2019-12-01
```

You have learned to deploy an API and its policy by using the Azure REST API. Compared to ARM templates and Azure Bicep, this approach is more flexible as it can be integrated into existing source code that supports HTTP. Furthermore, many developers are already familiar with other REST APIs. From my experience, learning the Azure REST API is not seen as a challenge by most developers and might therefore be a great choice for those developers that want to work with their language of choice.

Terraform

Terraform is an open source tool to manage infrastructure in Azure and other cloud providers. In fact, its great advantage over other infrastructure as code (IaC) tools is that it is cloud agnostic, which makes it a very popular tool in the cloud community.

The following Terraform file deploys the Demo Conference API and its policy to Azure API Management. It is split into three parts; part 1 sets the provider for interacting with Azure, part 2 defines the API, and part 3 defines the API policy.

Listing 11-14 shows how to set the Azure provider **azurerm**. You get the latest version of *azurerm* at the main directory of publicly available Terraform providers `https://registry.terraform.io/providers/hashicorp/azurerm/latest`.

Listing 11-14. Part 1 of the Terraform file for setting the Azure provider

```
terraform {
  required_providers {
    azurerm = {
      source  = "hashicorp/azurerm"
      version = "=2.67.0"
    }
  }
}

provider "azurerm" {
}
```

Listing 11-15 shows how to define an API resource. In Terraform, a resource is the most important element. A resource block describes one or more infrastructure objects, in our case, an API. The type of this resource element is `azurerm_api_management_api`; its local name `api`. The resource type and the local name together serve as the identifier that we can use to reference it.

Listing 11-15. Part 2 of the Terraform file defines an API

```
resource "azurerm_api_management_api" "api" {
  name                 = "demo-conference-api"
  resource_group_name  = "mastering-apim-rg"
  api_management_name  = "mastering-apim"
  revision             = "1"
  display_name         = "Demo Conference API"
  path                 = "conf"
  protocols            = ["https"]

  import {
    content_format = "swagger-link-json"
    content_value  = "http://conferenceapi.azurewebsites.net/?format=json"
  }
}
```

In Listing 11-16, we define the API policy resource element. The features reference the *api* resource element to get their values. To define the policy, it supports two options, `xml_content` for defining the policy code and `xml_link` which expects a URL to a publicly available policy file.

Listing 11-16. Part 3 of the Terraform file defines an API policy

```
resource "azurerm_api_management_api_policy" "api_policy" {
  api_name             = azurerm_api_management_api.api.name
  api_management_name  = azurerm_api_management_api.api.api_management_name
  resource_group_name  = azurerm_api_management_api.api.resource_group_name

  xml_content = <<XML
<policies>
  <inbound>
```

```
    <find-and-replace from="xyz" to="abc" />
  </inbound>
</policies>
XML
}
```

To initialize a Terraform project, create a working directory where you place your Terraform file and run the following command within the same directory:

```
terraform init
```

To see what Terraform will deploy or remove before it performs any change in Azure, run:

```
terraform plan
```

Terraform will describe in detail what happens before applying your Terraform file. Once you are ready to deploy your API and its policy, run:

```
terraform apply
```

You have now successfully deployed the Demo Conference API and its policy with Terraform.

Terraform has many providers such as for Amazon Web Service (AWS), Google Cloud Platform (GCP), Azure, and many more. It makes it a great IaC tool for organizations that manage resources in different cloud providers. My experience with managing Azure API Management with Terraform is that it does not support new features immediately. In fact, it took several months before the *Consumption* SKU was implemented. However, Terraform is a great choice as it is easy to get started with because of its detailed documentation and great user adoption.

Summary

You have learned to deploy APIs and policies in many ways, with the Azure CLI, Azure PowerShell module, ARM templates, Azure Bicep, Azure REST API, and the Azure provider in Terraform. You have also learned that there is no best way. A best way can only be one that fits your people and your ecosystem. You must decide what technology or tool works best for you, your team, or your organization. I know from my experience working in a cloud platform team – we were responsible for Azure API Management – that ARM templates did not work well for our application developers because they spend most of their day with high-level languages such as Java and C#. ARM is a technology they touch occasionally, so those developers required a lot of support from us. We were developing most of their ARM templates, which meant that those developers did not feel real ownership for their APIs. API ownership is something that we took very seriously, so we decided to create PowerShell scripts that everyone could use to deploy their APIs, policies, and products, accessible as tasks and task groups in Azure DevOps. We empowered our application developers to deploy to Azure API Management even though it was a black box for many of them. However, the future of infrastructure as code in Azure is not ARM templates anymore, it is Bicep where Microsoft puts in its effort.

Other teams in our organization were already deploying their databases and other Azure services with Terraform. Deploying APIs with the same tool might be an obvious choice.

CHAPTER 12

Power Apps

Power Apps allow citizen developers to build mobile-friendly apps quickly and without the need to implement traditional pro-code. While this low-code approach makes it easy to create custom apps quickly, a citizen developer might still need some support from you to connect the data from a web service and surface that data in a Power App.

Note Power Apps are part of a different pricing model, not related to Azure API Management. Read the documentation about Power Apps pricing.

In this chapter, you will learn to connect Azure API Management to the Power Platform. You will create a simple Power App from scratch and visualize a JSON response from an API that is hosted in Azure API Management. Figure 12-1 illustrates how a backend web service API can be altered on each level and so, create an API in Power Apps that is best suitable for your citizen developers.

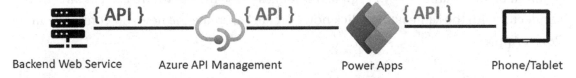

Figure 12-1. *APIs from the perspective of a citizen developer*

For example, an API in Power Apps might only contain a subset of all available endpoints that the connected API in Azure API Management exposes to simplify the use of it and to make the API more useable.

I created a simple Book API in Azure API Management with one operation **Book**. Listing 12-1 demonstrates the inbound policy of this operation. To keep it simple for this demonstration, the operation returns a JSON object with only one key/value pair.

© Sven Malvik 2022
S. Malvik, *Mastering Azure API Management*, https://doi.org/10.1007/978-1-4842-8011-9_12

Listing 12-1. API policy for the book operation

```
<inbound>
    <base />
    <return-response>
        <set-header name="Content-Type" exists-action="override">
            <value>application/json</value>
        </set-header>
        <set-body>
            {"Book" : "Mastering Azure API Management"}
        </set-body>
    </return-response>
</inbound>
```

Creating a Connection

To connect an API that is hosted in Azure API Management on the Power Platform can be achieved directly from the API in Azure API Management as Figure 12-2 illustrates. Click on the three dots on the right-hand side of the API you want to connect and select **Create Power Connector**. A new dialog opens where you name your new connector. Select a Power Apps environment that you want to use and give your API eventually a different display name in Power Apps; this makes sense in case where there is already a connector with the same name. Click now "Create" to create the new API connector in Power Apps.

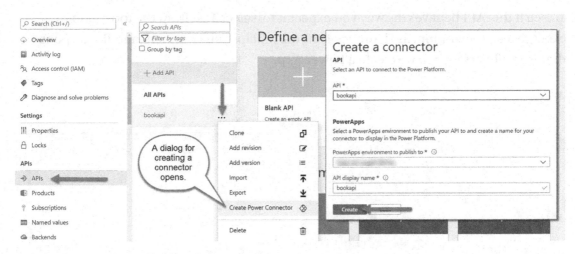

Figure 12-2. *Creating a connector to Power Apps*

Switch over to your Power Apps environment `https://make.powerapps.com/` to see your new connector; it is located under **Custom Connectors** that you find in the left-hand menu. Figure 12-3 shows a list of all custom connectors in your Power Apps environment. In this example, there is only one connector, "bookapi." To see all available operations of this connector, click the pen icon.

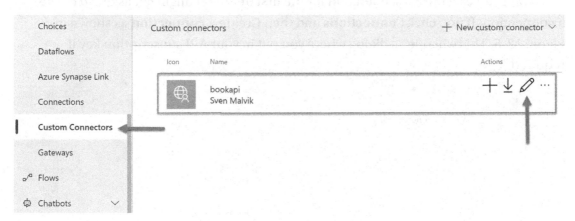

Figure 12-3. *List of custom connectors in Power Apps*

The pen icon opens an editor where you can adjust the API in Power Apps that is fronting your API in Azure API Management. Like policies in Azure API Management, you can add or remove operations, add default parameters to requests, or re-route calls.

To see if this API behaves the way you expect it to, select **Test** from the top menu to execute a test operation, as Figure 12-4 shows. It helps you to understand the response that we will parse when we create a Power App.

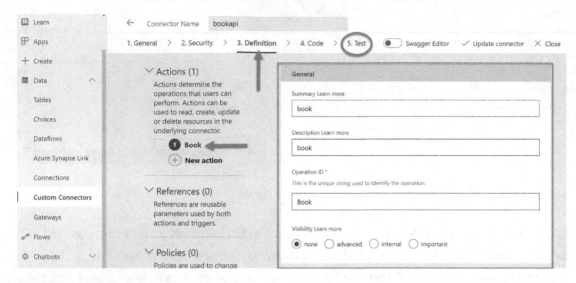

Figure 12-4. *Editing a custom connector*

When you execute a test operation for the first time, you might get asked to create a connection. If not, click **Connections** and then **Create a connection** as shown in Figure 12-5. This will open a dialog where you put in your API subscription key if required.

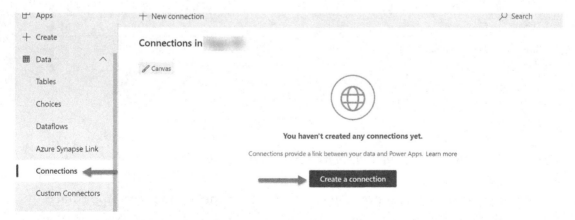

Figure 12-5. *Creating a connection*

You create a connection from a connector. There are already plenty of connectors for many services available, such as for SharePoint, DropBox, and many more. Figure 12-6 shows where you search for your custom connector by using the search field. Then click + on the right-hand side of your custom connector, in my case "bookapi," and click **Create** in the following dialog.

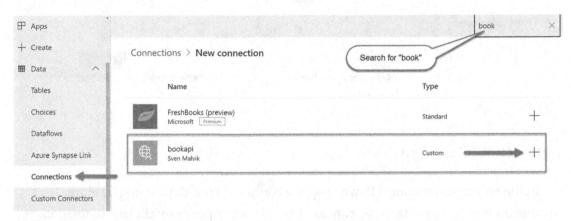

Figure 12-6. *Available connections*

Great, you have now a connection from your Power Apps environment to your API in Azure API Management, ready to use.

Creating a Power App

In this section, I want to show you to create a Power App and print out the value from the API response by using the connection that you created.

Click *Create* in the left-hand menu to create a **Canvas app from blank**. A dialog opens where you set an *App name* and a format. I selected *Tablet*, but it does not matter as we just want to print a value from an API. Click *Create* to open the Power App editor as shown in Figure 12-7.

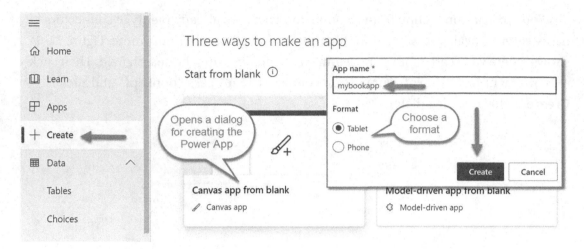

Figure 12-7. *Creating a Power App*

In the editor for creating a Power App, we connect to our data at first by either clicking on connect to data in the canvas of your Power App, or by clicking in the data source icon in the left-hand menu. As shown in Figure 12-8, a dialog with possible data sources opens. Select your "bookapi" connection.

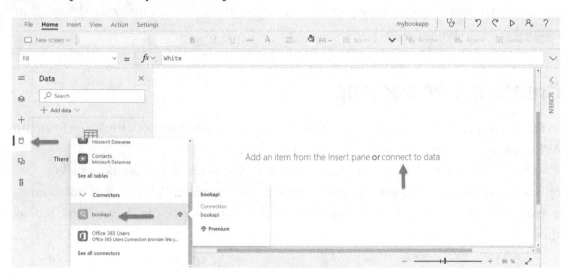

Figure 12-8. *Connecting the Power App with the API*

Your data is now accessible for your Power App. Add a label to the canvas of your Power App. We want to display the value from the Book API there. To read the value from the response of the Book API, you must create a formula.

In order to access this operation, you set the following formula for the label that you created:

```
bookapi.Book().Book
```

The first part of the formula bookapi is your connection which represents the Book API. The second part Book() represents the operation that we want to call, and the last part Book represents the key of the key/value pair of the JSON response. Remember, this is the response we have set in the policy for the **Book** operation:

```
{"Book" : "Mastering Azure API Management"}
```

Figure 12-9 demonstrates all steps for calling the Book API and displaying the response of the Book API on the canvas of your Power App.

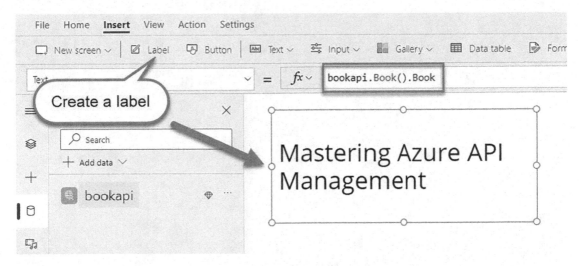

Figure 12-9. *Writing a formula for reading a value from the API*

Congratulations, you have created a Power App that displays data from an API by connecting to your Azure API Management instance.

Summary

In this chapter, you learned how to expose an API in Power Apps by connecting an API in Azure API Management to your Power Apps environment. You created then a simple Power App and used this API to display a value from a response.

Imagine if you would expose many of your APIs in Power Apps together with other sources such as Azure AD, SharePoint, or Excel, to mention just a few. It enables citizen developers to truly create powerful applications by combining data from across your entire organization.

PART IV

Enterprise Integration

CHAPTER 13

Networking

When you deploy Azure API Management with the default configuration for virtual networking, your instance will not be deployed into a virtual network (VNET), and thus be fully accessible from the Internet. This is a great way to share your public APIs with the world.

There are other use cases where you might not want to or can expose your APIs publicly and where you need to share your APIs with external partners or internal users only. You might have web APIs on-premises and want to expose them in Azure API Management in a hybrid cloud scenario where a secure connection with other vendors or datacenters is required. To achieve any of these use cases, you can deploy Azure API Management into a VNET.

There are three types of VNETs, none, internal, and external. *None* is the default configuration, as shown in Figure 13-1. Once deployed, you can switch from internal to external and vice versa later.

Home > Create a resource > API Management >

Create API Management ...

Basics   Monitoring   Scale   Managed identity   **Virtual network**   Protocol settings   Tags   Review + create

> ⓘ Securely access resources available in or through your Azure Virtual Network.

Type *
- ◉ None
- ◯ External
- ◯ Internal

Figure 13-1. *VNET types*

© Sven Malvik 2022
S. Malvik, *Mastering Azure API Management*, https://doi.org/10.1007/978-1-4842-8011-9_13

In this chapter, you will learn to secure Azure API Management without a VNET but also, when you should deploy Azure API Management into an *internal* or *external* VNET, so you understand how APIs will be exposed to your API consumers.

Note   VNET integration is only available in the Developer and Premium tier.

We will also look at how to integrate backend web services into Azure API Management as a load balancer for a multi-AKS-cluster that runs mission critical workload where you simply can't rely on one AKS cluster only.

Internal Virtual Network (VNET)

When you deploy Azure API Management into an internal VNET, by default, your APIs are inaccessible from outside this VNET because the API gateway does not have a public facing IP address. However, when you deploy Azure API Management into an internal VNET, you will get a public IP address. You can see this IP address in the *Overview* of your instance of Azure API Management as shown in Figure 13-2. This public IP address is only used for control plane traffic to the *management* endpoint which, that is, the Azure Resource Manager uses to manage configuration. You can lock this IP address down to the `ApiManagement` service tag.

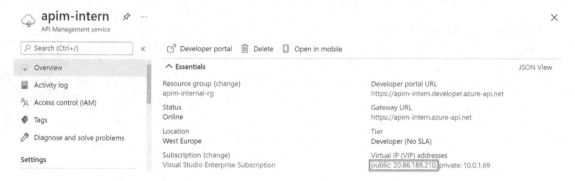

Figure 13-2. *Public IP address in internal VNET*

To sum it up, we have a public IP address for managing configuration and we have a private IP address for accessing the API gateway, developer portal, Git, and the management endpoint. However, when you call an API in Azure API Management from a virtual machine that is inside the same VNET or in a peered VNET by using the private

IP address, you receive a HTTP status code 503, service unavailable. This is because your API Management service does not listen to requests coming from IP addresses. It only responds to requests to the hostname configured on its service endpoints as shown in Figure 13-3.

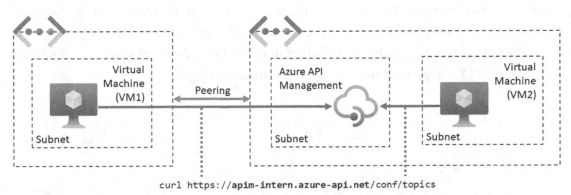

curl https://apim-intern.azure-api.net/conf/topics

Figure 13-3. *Calling Azure API Management in internal VNET mode*

At this point, the virtual machine (VM1) does not recognize the hostname apim-intern.azure-api, so calling an API fails at this point as Azure does not manage DNS for an internal VNET. To resolve this, you can map the host file. I created a virtual machine (VM1) with Ubuntu where the host file is located at /etc/hosts and added the following entry which contains the target IP address (the private IP address of Azure API Management) and the hostname for the API gateway:

10.0.1.69 apim-intern.azure-api.net

Another option for resolving the hostname is by configuring an Azure private DNS zone and linking it to the VNET where your Azure API Management instance is deployed described in the Azure documentation for private DNS.

The question you might ask is, how can I expose APIs together with the developer portal to my external API consumers. The short answer is by sending requests via a gateway. Azure Application Gateway is such a gateway that is commonly used in front of Azure API Management. It is a layer-7 load balancer and acts as a reverse proxy which has a public IP address, of course, and a built-in Web Application Firewall (WAF); Azure API Management does not provide WAF. In a nutshell, if you run mission critical web services that can be accessed via Azure API Management and you decide to lock down your instance into an internal VNET, using Azure Application Gateway is a recommended PaaS service to protect your infrastructure from malicious requests.

Figure 13-4 illustrates how to protect Azure API Management in an internal VNET with Azure Application Gateway in front. As Azure API Management does not provide a public IP address for the API gateway, external API consumers send requests to the external endpoint of Azure Application Gateway. Depending on the URL format you set up, Azure Application Gateway sends the requests to your Azure API Management instance or eventually to a different backend that you have in place such as an Azure App Service where you run a landing website that does not need the overhead that comes with Azure API Management such as subscriptions and API policies.

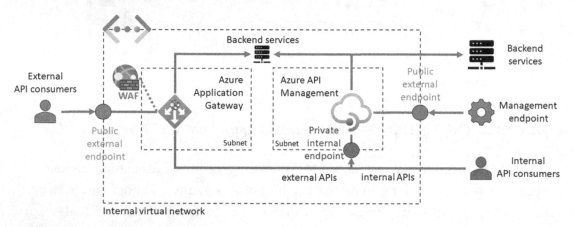

Figure 13-4. *Azure API Management in an internal VNET*

Internal API consumers can access the internal endpoint directly if those requests come from a VNET that is peered with the VNET where Azure API Management is deployed in because Azure API Management deployed in internal mode provides only a private IP address for the API gateway.

Note   API Management service does not listen to requests coming from IP addresses. It only responds to requests to the hostname configured on its service endpoints.

When you deploy Azure API Management into an existing subnet of a VNET, make sure that your Network Security Group (NSG) – if you have one associated with the subnet – opens for some necessary ports that Azure API Management needs. You find a list of all required ports in the documentation for common network configuration issues.

External VNET

When you deploy Azure API Management into an external VNET, by default, your APIs are exposed on the Internet as the API gateway provides a public facing IP address as Figure 13-5 shows.

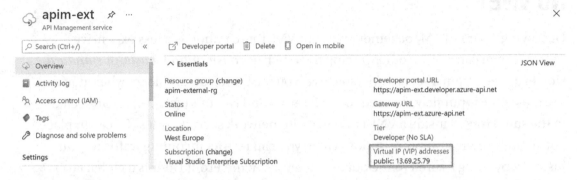

Figure 13-5. *Public IP address in external VNET*

However, even though your APIs are publicly exposed on the Internet, you can still restrict incoming traffic by associating a Network Security Group to the subnet of your Azure API Management instance as shown in Figure 13-6.

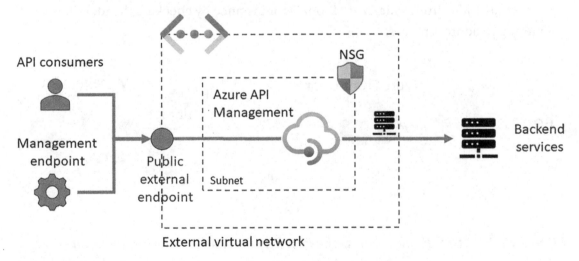

Figure 13-6. *Azure API Management in an external VNET*

For example, instead of using Azure Application Gateway in front of Azure API Management as suggested for the internal mode, using the global Azure Front Door gateway as a layer-7 load balancer which has near real-time failover requires a backend – in this case Azure API Management – to provide a public IP address. With Azure API Management in external mode, you have a public IP address where you can configure NSG rules to restrict incoming traffic to Azure Front Door only.

No VNET

Deploying Azure API Management without VNET integration is a less expensive option as you can choose other pricing tiers such as *consumption*, *basic*, or *standard*. However, seen from a security perspective, you are more vulnerable to cyberattacks as your instance is publicly exposed to the Internet and can therefore not be protected in the same way as inside a VNET/subnet with network security rules (NSGs) in place. Fortunately, there is another option where you can restrict incoming traffic to your instance by using Azure Front Door as a gateway. Azure Front Door is a global layer-7 load balancer and comes with a Web Application Firewall (WAF), so your Azure API Management instance is better protected against cyber-attacks from the public Internet than without.

Figure 13-7 illustrates how you can restrict the public endpoint of Azure API Management without VNET integration. The idea is to implement a policy that restricts the incoming traffic from your Azure Front Door instance by checking the identifier and by filtering IP address ranges.

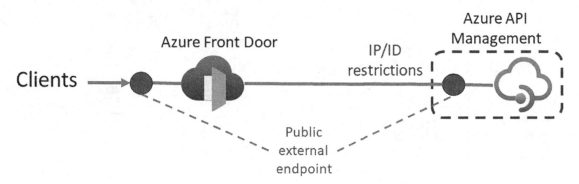

Figure 13-7. *Azure Front Door as the gateway for Azure API Management*

Microsoft Azure updates weekly its IP address ranges for Azure, its regions, as well as several Azure services such as Azure Logic Apps and Azure Front Door. You can download the JSON file and extract all IP ranges for Azure Front Door that you find in the section with the name `AzureFrontDoor.Backend`. You know when there has been a change in IP address ranges by watching the property changeNumber, as shown in the following:

```json
{
  "name": "AzureFrontDoor.Backend",
  "id": "AzureFrontDoor.Backend",
  "properties": {
    "changeNumber": 7,
    "region": "",
    "regionId": 0,
    "platform": "Azure",
    "systemService": "",
    "addressPrefixes": [
      "13.73.248.16/29",
      "20.21.37.40/29",
      "..."
    ]
  }
}
```

The JSON file defines IP address ranges as addressPrefixes, so you must convert them to address ranges first in order to use them in Azure API Management policies. As an example, the address prefix 13.73.248.16/29 converts into the address range from 13.73.248.17 to 13.73.248.22.

A policy for IP address ranges looks like the following example that you can place in the global policy of Azure API Management, so all APIs can inherit it:

```xml
<inbound>
    <ip-filter action="allow">
        <address-range from="13.73.248.17" to="13.73.248.22" />
        <address-range from="20.21.37.41" to="20.21.37.46" />
        <address-range from="..." to="..." />
    </ip-filter>
</inbound>
```

The second part of restricting incoming traffic to your Azure API Management instance is by checking the identifier (ID) of your Azure Front Door instance. You can find the *Front Door ID* in the overview of your Azure Front Door instance, as shown in Figure 13-8.

Figure 13-8. *Azure Front Door ID*

Azure Front Door sets a header `X-Azure-FDID` in all requests that you can check by using the `check-header` policy and setting the Front Door ID as the value, as shown in the following:

```
<inbound>
    <check-header name="X-Azure-FDID" failed-check-httpcode="403"
    failed-check-error-message="access denied" ignore-case="false">
        <value>{FRONTDOOR_ID}</value>
    </check-header>
</inbound>
```

Set the value as a named value in Azure API Management, so you can easily change it later if you should switch to another Azure Front Door instance.

You can use Azure Front Door as a gateway toward Azure API Management also in case where you have your instance in external mode and want to restrict the traffic.

Backend Integration with AKS

We use Azure API Management as a façade toward our backend web services that can come in different technologies, locations, and requirements. Some backend web services run as containers inside an Azure Kubernetes Service (AKS); others need to be combined in order to form a meaningful API; and some backend web services even run outside our Azure tenant, on-premises.

Kubernetes is an open source platform for container orchestration. Azure Kubernetes Service (AKS) is designed for organizations that want to build scalable applications with Docker and Kubernetes while using the Azure architecture. It helps to manage a lot of cluster management such as reducing the complexity of deployment and management tasks, but also upgrading Kubernetes itself which you can do by executing the following command:

```
az aks upgrade \
    --resource-group myResourceGroup \
    --name myAKScluster \
    --kubernetes-version KUBERNETES_VERSION
```

As simple as it seems, it comes with a risk. In my organization, we experienced problems multiple times during an upgrade of AKS itself, where we had to involve Microsoft's support team to help us out with nodes that began to hang, one by one. Depending on your support level, solving a problem may take some time where your Kubernetes cluster might not process requests as it happened to us. To reduce risks like this, you may consider deploying applications in multiple AKS clusters to improve availability, isolation, and scalability. I want to discuss one approach of running multiple AKS clusters behind Azure API Management that we successfully use.

Policy-managed load balancing is where a policy in Azure API Management decides to what AKS cluster to send requests to. This approach does not introduce additional Azure services and seems therefore to be less complex and easy to manage. However, a policy is code that you write and maintain which adds complexity to the overall system that you manage which itself adds risk.

Figure 13-9 illustrates Azure API Management as a load balancer in front of two AKS clusters. The idea is to weight the amount of traffic sent to one or another AKS cluster. Imagine that you want to upgrade the upper blue AKS cluster. To verify that the upgrade was successful, you start routing just a small amount of traffic to the newly upgraded AKS cluster and observe its behavior by analyzing the logs and looking for abnormal behavior. If everything looks normal, you increase the amount of traffic until it reaches the value that is suitable for this AKS cluster depending on the number and type of its underlying VMs, in this case 40%.

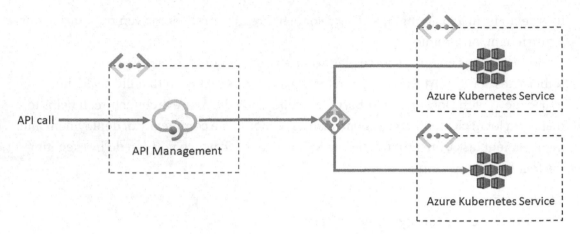

Figure 13-9. *Azure API Management as a load balancer*

An implementation of the weights of participating AKS clusters looks like shown in Listing 13-1. A named value `clusters` defines a list of clusters where each element has at least two values, an identifier, in this case a color, and a percentage value.

Listing 13-1. Weighted AKS clusters as named value in Azure API Management

```
{ {"blue","40"}, {"green","100"} }
```

The first element in the list that has the identifier *blue* receives 40% of the traffic while the second element *green* receives 60%, `value of element[i-1] - value of element[i]`. This allows for additional clusters by adding more elements to the list without changing the implementation of a policy that uses those values.

Listing 13-2 shows an example of the global policy for weighted load balancing between multiple AKS clusters that uses the named value `{{clusters}}`. The policy does two things; it sets a variable `aksBackendUrl` in the *inbound* section and it forwards the request to the backend.

Remember   An effective policy is the result of the policies of all scopes, operation, API, product, and global.

The policy sets a random number between 0 and 100. The idea with this number is to match the number with an element in the list to send a request to. As an example, the number 70 matches the second element *green* as it is between the two values 40 and 100. To find this element, I iterate through the list using a linear search and check whether the random value is between the previous and the current element; the first iteration is a bit special as it does not have a previous element. Once I have found a match, I return it by creating the URL of AKS using this identifier of the matched element and store it in aksBackendUrl.

Listing 13-2. Global policy for weighted load balancing

```
<policies>
    <inbound>
        <set-variable name="aksBackendUrl" value="@{
            int rnd = new Random().Next(100);
            string[,] clusters = {{clusters}};

            for (int i = 0; i <= servers.GetUpperBound(0); i++) {
                if (i == 0) {
                    if (rnd <= Int16.Parse(clusters[i,1])) {
                        return "http://aks-" + clusters[i,0] +
                        ".azurecloud.no";
                    }
                } else if (rnd > Int16.Parse(clusters[i-1,1]) && rnd <=
                Int16.Parse(clusters[i,1])) {
                    return "http://aks-" + clusters[i,0] + ".
                    azurecloud.no";
                } else {
                // rnd is not withing the range for this cluster
                }
            }
            // Return primary clusters
            return "http://aks-" + clusters[0,0] + ". azurecloud.no";
        }" />
    </inbound>
    <backend>
        <forward-request />
    </backend>
    <outbound />
    <on-error />
</policies>
```

I use the variable aksBackendUrl in API policies to set the backend service URL. As you can see in Listing 13-3, I put <base /> in the beginning of the inbound section to insert upper scoped policies such as the global policy where I set this variable.

Listing 13-3. API policy

```
<inbound>
    <base />
    <set-backend-service base-url="@(context.Variables.GetValueOrDefault
    ("aksBackendUrl", "{{AKSBackendUrl}}") + context.Api.Path)" />
</inbound>
```

Let us assume that the code of the global policy does not work as intended and aksBackendUrl is not set. In this case, I return a default value which I set as an ordinary named value by using this context.Variables.GetValueOrDefault(VALUE, DEVAULT_VALUE).

Summary

In this chapter, you learned to integrate Azure API Management into a VNET. We discussed when it makes sense to use what VNET mode, internal or external, and that it depends on your use case. Not all use cases require a VNET integration. You might want to expose your APIs publicly on the Internet, so all developers can subscribe to them without any restrictions. Other uses cases may require a highly secured Azure API Management instance where an internal VNET integration is the only option. As you have learned in this chapter, publicly exposed APIs can be secured.

I hope that I could give you enough insight into Azure API Management and VNET integration, so you can make good architectural decisions in the future.

## CHAPTER 14

Self-hosted API Gateway

When you call an API in Azure API Management, the request is handled by the managed API gateway component of your instance, which then forwards the requests to a backend web service. In cases where a backend web service is hosted nearby and the traffic is going via the Azure backbone, this is fine because latency is kept to a minimum and security to a maximum. However, there are other cases where backend web services are hosted outside of your Azure tenant and where the traffic to backend web services goes via the public Internet and not via the Azure backbone. Those cases can not only be challenging security-wise as data is sent out of the network but might also break compliance policies of an organization where traffic must stay local.

Figure 14-1 illustrates the connectivity between API consumers and backend web services using the managed API gateway of an Azure API Management instance. The managed API gateway is hosted at the same location as your Azure API Management instance. All traffic goes through this centralized component no matter where backend web services are hosted, on-premise and far away from your Azure API Management instance or hosted at another cloud provider where you might legally not be able to send out requests from. If your backend web services are hosted near your Azure API Management instance, this should be fine. For example, I worked in a project where we hosted Azure API Management and Azure Kubernetes Service – we ran all backend web services there – in the same VNET. A managed API gateway is everything we needed. Latency was kept to a minimum as both services were deployed at the same location; security was strengthened through network security rules of the subnets; and compliancy was ensured as compliance rules were the same.

© Sven Malvik 2022
S. Malvik, *Mastering Azure API Management*, https://doi.org/10.1007/978-1-4842-8011-9_14

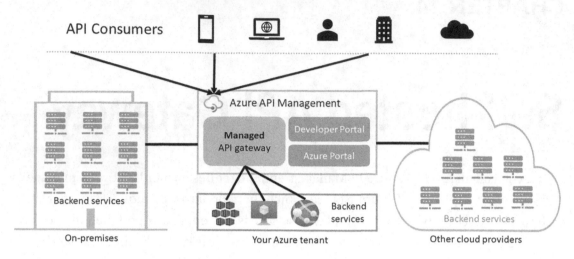

Figure 14-1. *Managed API gateway*

In a hybrid world where backend web services run in different locations, Azure, on-premises, or other cloud providers, a managed API gateway might not always be a good solution. Luckily, Azure API Management lets you run the API gateway near your backend web services using a self-hosted API gateway.

API consumers call APIs of a self-hosted gateway instead of the managed API gateway. Technically, this means that an API consumer can descide whether to call an API in a self-hosted or the managed API gateway; both work at the same time.

Figure 14-2 illustrates the connectivity between API consumers and backend web services using both, self-hosted API gateways and the managed API gateway of an Azure API Management instance. Compared to the managed API gateway, traffic from an API consumer to a backend web service that is hosted outside your Azure tenant can travel directly to the backend services, which results in lower latency. The illustration also shows two dashed lines between Azure API Management and the self-hosted API gateways. A self-hosted API gateway uses this connection over port 443 to communicate its status, sends request logs and metrics to Azure Monitor, but also applies configuration updates such as adding or deleting an API to or from a self-hosted API gateway. If the connection is broken, the self-hosted API gateway can't start.

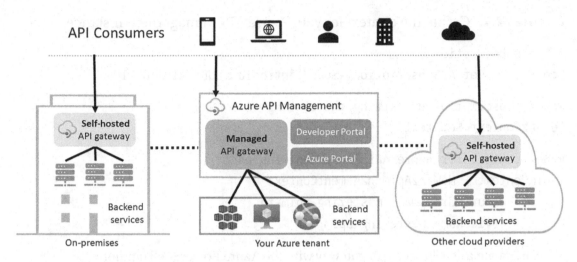

Figure 14-2. *Self-hosted API gateway*

Note   Self-hosted API gateways are only available in the *Developer* and *Premium* pricing tiers.

A self-hosted API gateway needs a container orchestration solution such as Docker or Kubernetes to run, as self-hosted API gateways are Linux-based Docker containers.

Creating a Self-hosted API Gateway

You can create multiple self-hosted API gateways which are useful for different backend web services. You might have legacy backend web services running on-premises that cover a certain domain or speaking in Azure API Management terms, product. In this case, you might want to create an API gateway that includes only APIs that are within this product. Once you eventually migrate a certain backend web service to another runtime environment, you can remove this API from the self-hosted API gateway and add it to another self-hosted API gateway where the migrated backend web services run, all without redeploying the self-hosted API gateways.

Before we create an API gateway from an Azure API Management instance, we need to create a $apimContext variable that describes the instance, as Listing 14-1 describes.

Listing 14-1. Create the context for your Azure API Management instance.

```
# Get subscription
$context = Get-AzSubscription -SubscriptionId <SUBSCRIPTION_ID>

# Set subscription by setting the context
Set-AzContext $context

# Set context for Azure API Management instance
$apimContext = New-AzApiManagementContext `
    -ResourceGroupName mastering-apim-rg `
    -ServiceName mastering-apim
```

You create a self-hosted API gateway with the Azure PowerShell cmdlet New-AzApiManagementGateway. It requires metadata pertaining to the resource geographic location. The cmdlet does not really need any data, a name is the only requirement, as the following code shows:

```
$location = New-AzApiManagementResourceLocationObject -Name loc
```

Listing 14-2 lists two PowerShell cmdlets for creating a functional self-hosted API gateway, New-AzApiManagementGateway for creating the API gateway and Add-AzApiManagementApiToGateway for adding an API to it using the ApiId parameter. Both cmdlets require the $apimContext variable.

Listing 14-2. Creating a self-hosted API gateway with Azure PowerShell

```
# Creates a new self-hosted API gateway
New-AzApiManagementGateway -Context $apimContext -GatewayId
myGateway -LocationData $location

# Adds an API to the gateway
Add-AzApiManagementApiToGateway -Context $apimContext -GatewayId
myGateway -ApiId ConferenceApi
```

You can run Add-AzApiManagementApiToGateway as many times as you have APIs in Azure API Management. Once your self-hosted API gateway includes your APIs, it is available from the Microsoft Container Registry. To check this, you could list all available self-hosted API gateways by running the Get-AzApiManagementGateway cmdlet.

```
Get-AzApiManagementGateway -Context $apimContext -GatewayId myGateway
```

As you created only one self-hosted API gateway for now, you see one entry with the gateway identifier (*GatewayId*) myGateway.

Deploying a Self-hosted API Gateway

You learned from the previous section that a self-hosted API gateway comes as a Docker image mcr.microsoft.com/azure-api-management/gateway:latest. To successfully deploy the image as a container, it depends on two configurations, the **service endpoint**, and an **authorization token**. In this section, I will demonstrate how you can retrieve both values and then deploy your self-hosted API gateway to a local Ubuntu environment that has Docker already preinstalled.

Configuration

There are at least two options for getting the configurations, manually from the Azure portal or programmatically by using PowerShell. If you want to run the self-hosted API gateway in a production environment, you should choose the latter as the authorization token has a maximum lifetime of 30 days, so you need to repeat the steps after approximately one month.

Service Endpoint

Start off by creating a context variable $apimContext, as Listing 14-1 describes. You might still have it in memory, so you might want to skip this. You can use the context variable to create the first part of the first configuration, the service ID by running the following code:

```
$serviceId = Get-AzApiManagement | select -expand id
```

Alternatively, you can set the service ID manually; it will not change later. As you can see, it contains only static values, the subscription ID, and the service name of your Azure API Management instance.

```
$serviceId = "/subscriptions/<SUBSCRIPTION_ID>/resourceGroups/mastering-apim-rg/providers/Microsoft.ApiManagement/service/<SERVICE_NAME>"
```

The second part is the service endpoint itself. Create it by introducing a $SERVICE_ ENDPOINT variable and store its value, as shown in the following:

```
$SERVICE_ENDPOINT = `
        "https://mastering-apim.management.azure-api.net" + `
        $serviceId + `
        "?api-version=2021-01-01-preview"
```

Authorization Token

The second configuration is the authorization token for the self-hosted API gateway. You generate this token by sending a POST request generateToken of the gateway resource; it is represented by its resource identifier. You can read the resource identifier $id of the self-hosted API gateway either by using Azure PowerShell or by setting it manually. As it is a static value, that will never change, both approaches are fine. To get the gateway ID, use the Azure PowerShell cmdlet Get-AzApiManagementGateway together with the context from Listing 14-1 and the gateway name myGateway. Filter the result with select -expand to retrieve the gateway ID.

```
$id = Get-AzApiManagementGateway `
        -Context $apimContext `
        -GatewayId myGateway `
        | select -expand id
```

The gateway ID is a static string containing your subscription ID, the service name, and the name of the self-hosted API gateway.

```
/subscriptions/<SUBSCRIPTION_ID>/resourceGroups/mastering-apim-rg/
providers/Microsoft.ApiManagement/service/mastering-apim/
gateways/<GATEWAY_NAME>
```

Use the gateway ID to create the URL for generating an authorization token and store it in a value $url, as shown in the following:

```
$url = "https://management.azure.com/" + $id + "/generateToken/?
api-version=2019-12-01"
```

As you are sending a POST request to $url, you need a payload in JSON format which defines the key type, and an expiring date. A token cannot be valid for more than 30 days before it must be regenerated. That is why there are two key types, primary or secondary. A self-hosted API gateway uses the secondary key when the primary key changes after 30 days; the same is true when the secondary key must be regenerated. Set $expiry to 30 days from now using the following code example:

```
$expiryDate = (Get-date).AddDays(30)
$expiry = Get-Date $expiryDate -Format s
```

Once $expiry contains a value like mine, 2021-10-06T09:13:59, you can set the following JSON object to $bodyToken.

```
$bodyToken="{
        'keyType': 'primary',
        'expiry': '$expiry'
}"
```

Note   Set the key type to primary or secondary depending on which key expires first.

It is time to request the authorization token by using the Azure CLI command az rest, as demonstrated in the following. The response of this call is in JSON format. I use the popular command-line JSON processor jq to extract the actual token from it.

```
$TOKEN = az rest `
    --method POST `
    --uri "$url" `
    --body $bodyToken `
    | jq .value
```

Listing 14-3 shows the content of env.conf. This file contains both configurations, the service endpoint and the authorization token. Make sure to place the file on the same host on which you want to run your self-hosted API gateway.

Listing 14-3. The env.conf file contains two configurations.

```
config.service.endpoint=<paste SERVICE_ENDPOINT here>
config.service.auth=GatewayKey <paste TOKEN here>
```

For the purpose of this demonstration, I created `env.conf` on an Ubuntu VM.

Deployment

The final step for running a self-hosted API gateway is by creating a Docker container `myGateway` of the image `mcr.microsoft.com/azure-api-management/gateway:latest`. It requires two ports, *80* for accessing the APIs that are hosted by this gateway, and *443* as the configuration management channel where the self-hosted API gateway gets its updates and sends metrics over. You also give it the configuration file `env.conf`. If you prefer to set the configuration directly as parameters, you can do so using the parameter `--env` twice of each configuration instead of `--env-file`.

```
docker run \
    --detach \
    --name myGateway \
    --publish 80:8080 \
    --publish 443:8081 \
    --env-file env.conf \
    mcr.microsoft.com/azure-api-management/gateway:latest
```

Once you have executed the command, check if the container started successfully using `docker ps` to list all running containers and look for your container `myGateway`.

Until now, you have sent request to the managed API gateway using the following URL: `https://mastering-apim.azure-api.net/conf/topics`. By using the self-hosted API gateway from your machine, you can replace this with either `localhost` or the IP address of your machine, as demonstrated here:

```
curl localhost/conf/topics
```

This request gives you the usual response from the *Demo Conference API*.

Updating the Self-hosted API Gateway

As the development of our backend web services continues and the APIs change, we want to keep our self-hosted API gateways in sync. To ensure that our self-hosted APIs are in sync with the managed API gateway, Azure API Management requires a proper connection to the service instance over port *443*, the configuration management channel. In case you deployed Azure API Management in internal VNET mode, you must ensure that this port is open in the outbound directions so APIs can be added, deleted, or updated. As an example, delete the Demo Conference API *ConferenceApi* from the self-hosted API gateway *myGateway* by using the Azure PowerShell cmdlet `Delete-AzApiManagementApiToGateway` as shown in the following:

```
Delete-AzApiManagementApiToGateway `
      -Context $apimContext `
      -GatewayId myGateway `
      -ApiId ConferenceApi
```

This change removes an API immediately from your self-hosted API gateway and can't be called by API consumers anymore.

Summary

In this chapter, we discussed self-hosted API gateways. You learned that even though you manage self-hosted API gateways by yourself, there are certain use cases where they are a preferred option. For example, if your APIs are consumed by internal users only, keeping the traffic internally within the same network makes sense for several reasons: reduced latency, minimal bandwidth costs, and improved security.

You learned then to create a self-hosted API gateway programmatically by using Azure PowerShell. This is the preferable option in a production environment as the authorization token that is used to gain access to your Azure API Management instance is time limited to a maximum of 30 days. To renew this token, you should automate the process of generating this token using the code in this chapter.

At the end of this chapter, you deployed a Docker container for the self-hosted API gateway on a local machine, in this case an Ubuntu VM.

PART V

Maintenance

## CHAPTER 15

Security

You have learned many of the most important security aspects of Azure API Management already. However, there is at least one aspect remaining that you need to understand, authentication. In this chapter, you will learn to authenticate a client with a backend web service using both HTTP basic authentication and OAuth 2.0. At the end of this chapter, you will learn about two additional security aspects that are important to understand when working with Azure API Management.

Authentication

In this section, you will learn two ways of authenticating a client with a backend, HTTP basic authentication and OAuth 2.0.

HTTP Basic Authentication to Backend Web Services

HTTP basic authentication is the simplest technique for enforcing access controls to your backend web services as it does not require session identifiers or cookies. Instead, HTTP basic authentication uses the `Authorization` HTTP header field with username and password in plaintext, as shown in the following:

```
curl -H 'Authorization: Basic $(echo -n <YOUR_USERNAME>:<YOUR_PASSWORD> |
base64)' <YOUR_WEBSITE>
```

Username and password are base64 encoded, which can easily be decoded by an attacker in the same way the credentials are encoded. It makes this authentication method vulnerable in a couple of ways such as man-in-the-middle attacks and larger attack windows as this header must be included in all requests.

Figure 15-1 illustrates an end-to-end request with Azure API Management between an API consumer and a backend web service with HTTP basic authentication enabled.

© Sven Malvik 2022
S. Malvik, *Mastering Azure API Management*, https://doi.org/10.1007/978-1-4842-8011-9_15

An API consumer calls an Azure API Management hosted API – in this case, *Basic API* – with its subscription key to verify if the API consumer is allowed to access this API. The API then adds an *Authorization* header to the request in its policy before it gets forwarded to the backend web service, in this example, an Nginx website that is hosted on an Ubuntu virtual machine (VM) in Azure.

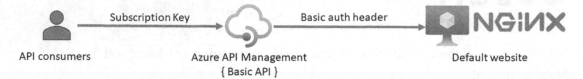

Figure 15-1. *HTTP basic authentication*

Let us start from the right site of Figure 15-1 and configure an Nginx web server with HTTP basic authentication enabled. If you have not installed an Nginx web server yet but would like to, you can follow the instructions in the official Nginx documentation.

Open your Nginx configuration file of your Nginx service /etc/nginx/sites-available/default. We want all pages from root to be secured; define this in the location / section, as Listing 15-1 shows. To enable basic authentication, add two directives, auth_basic and auth_basic_user_file. The first directive auth_basic sets the name for a dialog window which is shown in a browser if an *Authorization* header is missing in the request. The second directive auth_basic_user_file defines the path to the user/password file. All users in this file will have access to the defined location, in this case, all pages.

Listing 15-1. Nginx with HTTP basic authentication

```
location / {
    try_files $uri $uri/ =404;
    auth_basic "Restricted content";
    auth_basic_user_file /etc/nginx/.htpasswd;
}
```

Restart your Nginx service and try to access it from a browser to verify that a dialog window with the name "Restricted content" is shown.

Create a new API with an operation that you point to your Nginx web server; I named this API *Basic API* and the operation *test,* as shown in Figure 15-2. Set the context path *API URL suffix* to /basicapi. You can either disable the subscription key under *Settings* or make sure that your user has access to one.

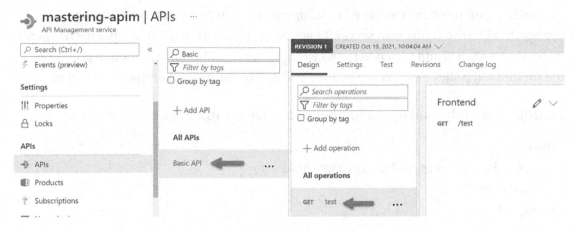

Figure 15-2. *HTTP basic authentication API demo*

Open the API policy and add the code from Listing 15-2. It defines the *inbound* section where you set the IP address – or URL if you have – in your Nginx web server. Set the address as a named value so you can change it easily later. All request to this API will now be forwarded to the Nginx web server. What is missing is the authorization header with the credentials. Use the predefined `authentication-basic` policy for this purpose and set both a username and a password.

Listing 15-2. Inbound API policy for basic authentication

```
<inbound>
    <set-backend-service base-url="{{backendUrl}}" />
    <authentication-basic username="{{basicUser}}"
    password="{{basicPassword}}" />
    <base />
</inbound>
```

As all requests will be using the same credentials, you might consider adding a technical user to your Nginx web server that is shared across all requests.

Remember   Your users are still identified by their individual subscription keys, so a shared technical user for a backend web service won't change this.

To dive a bit more into Azure API Management policies, I created a new page /mypage.html to the Nginx web server. To access this page from the new operation, open the policy test and add the code from Listing 15-3 to the inbound section. It contains the predefined policy rewrite-uri where you set the path to the endpoint in Nginx.

Listing 15-3. Inbound operation policy for basic authentication

```
<inbound>
    <rewrite-uri template="/mypage.html" />
    <base />
</inbound>
```

Now that you have created a new API in Azure API Management which forwards requests to your Nginx web server with basic authentication enabled, you might want to try it out. You do so by sending a cURL request to the endpoint in Azure API Management with your subscription key as you would normally do:

```
curl -H "Apikey: <YOUR_SUBSCRIPTION_KEY>" https://mastering-apim.azure-api.net/basicapi/test
```

When a request is processed in the effective policy, an authorization header with your base64-encoded username/password is added and forwarded to Nginx. The result is the content of mypage.html.

Authentication with OAuth 2.0

In the official documentation for OAuth 2.0, the following is stated: *"The OAuth 2.0 authorization framework is a protocol that allows a user to grant a third-party web site or application access to the user's protected resources, without necessarily revealing their long-term credentials or even their identity."*

Azure API Management supports authentication with OAuth 2.0. Its protected resources are the backend web applications that a third-party client application, such as the developer portal in Azure API Management, wants to access through APIs.

The developer portal – or any other third-party client application – requests an access token from the Azure Active Directory (Azure AD) using an *App registration client id* and a *client secret*. A user signs in with their credentials. Azure AD will then issue an access token that the user must add to an API call before an Azure API Management policy validates it.

Figure 15-3 illustrates a high-level view on how Azure AD relates to its registered applications and APIs in Azure API Management. There are three parts involved in this process, client, backend, and authentication server. The client – in this example, the developer portal in Azure API Management – is represented by a registered *Client App* in Azure AD. An API in Azure API Management is represented by a registered *Backend App* in Azure AD. To call an API from the developer portal, the client app needs to be granted permission to the backend app. Furthermore, the client app needs a secret so it can sign an access token that a request must contain.

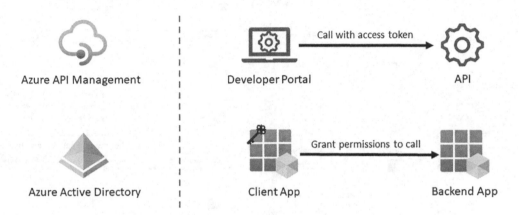

Figure 15-3. *Azure Active Directory App registrations*

I have divided the section in three parts for configuring Azure API Management with OAuth 2.0, Backend App, Client App, and Azure API Management.

Backend App

An API is represented as a *Backend App* in Azure AD. Search for Azure Active Directory in the Azure portal and click *App registrations,* as shown in Figure 15-4. Continue by clicking *New registration* to register a new application and name it backend-app. You are prompted to specify an **Application ID URI** like https://azurecloud.no/api which must be globally unique. If you don't set this value, a default value in the form api://<application-client-id> is provided.

Depending on your environment, you may want to let user accounts from other directories access the backend. In this example, I only support user accounts that are within this directory. After you clicked *Register*, the new application gets an **Application (client) id**. You will need this *client id* later when you implement an API policy to verify the callers access token.

Figure 15-4. *Registering the Backend App in Azure AD*

Add now a scope with a name. The **Scope name** is included in the access token of a request that an API policy can verify and eventually accept or reject. A common scope naming convention is `resource.operation.constraint`, so you may name the scope like `Users.Read.All`; I named mine *apis.full,* as shown in Figure 15-5. Make sure that you set an easy-to-understand description as users that sign in will be prompted with a consent dialog.

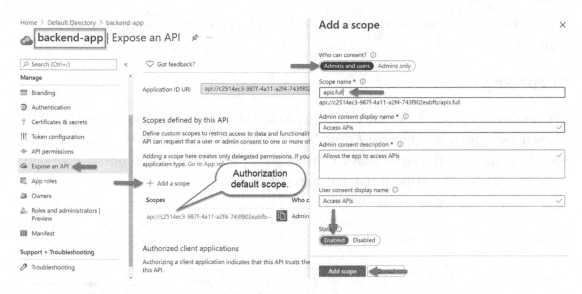

Figure 15-5. *Setting the scope of the backend app*

The version of the access token for the backend-app is currently set to *1*. Change the value of `accessTokenAcceptedVersion` to *2* as you want to use OAuth 2.0. Click **Manifest** in the left-hand menu to open the manifest of the Azure AD backend app and search for the term, as shown in Figure 15-6.

Figure 15-6. *Manifest of backend-app in Azure AD*

You have now created a representation of an API in the form of an application in Azure AD.

Client App

The developer portal, or any other client application that calls an API in Azure API Management, is represented as a *Client App* in Azure AD. Register a new application with the name client-app as shown in Figure 15-7. Depending on the context, you select the right option of the supported account types.

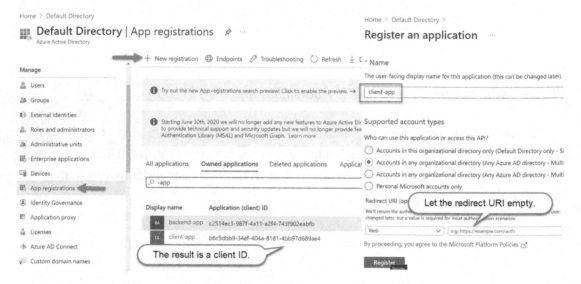

Figure 15-7. *Registering the Client App in Azure AD*

In the next step, you create a **Client Secret** which is used to authenticate the client's identity. When the developer portal requests an access token from Azure AD, it passes an authorization code along with authentication details, including the *client secret*, to an API token endpoint. The access token is a Json Web Token (JWT) with a signature hash.

Create a new client secret by navigating to *Certificates & secrets* in your client app client-app and click *New client secret*. Give it a name and set an expiration date. Click *Add* to create the client secret and secret value, as shown in Figure 15-8.

Figure 15-8. *Creating a client secret*

Grant the client app permission to call the backend app for signed-in users by following the steps shown in Figure 15-9. Navigate to *API permissions* on the left-hand side of your client app and click **Add a permission**. Select your backend app `backend-app` from the list of *My APIs* and mark the right permission. As you only created one permission, the list only contains `apis.full`. The permission is part of the access token that you send along with an API request from the developer portal, so it can be verified in a policy.

Figure 15-9. *Granting permissions to allow client-app to call backend-app*

You are not done with configuring the client-app yet. There is one setting missing that you get from your Azure API Management instance.

Azure API Management Instance Settings

In this section, you will enable user authorization with the OAuth 2.0 service in Azure API Management from the Azure portal. Navigate to *App registration* in Azure AD and click *Endpoints*. There are two endpoints that interest us, *OAuth 2.0 authorization endpoint (v2)* and *OAuth 2.0 token endpoint (v2)*; both are marked in Figure 15-10. Copy both URLs and paste them into your favorite text editor, so you have them at hand. We don't need the other URLs, so you can just ignore them.

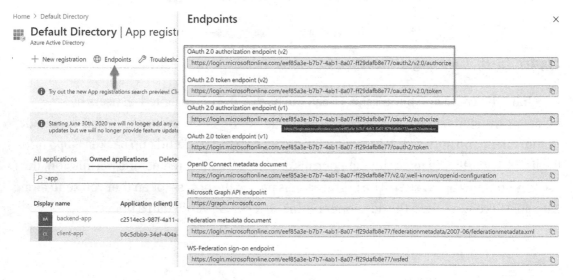

Figure 15-10. *OAuth 2.0 endpoints*

I named the OAuth 2.0 service that you will configure as *apim-oauth-service*. Navigate to your Azure API Management instance and click *OAuth 2.0 + OpenID Connect* in the left-hand menu followed by *Add* as you want to configure an OAuth 2.0 service. A new configuration window "Add OAuth 2 service" pops up on the right side, as shown in Figure 15-11.

I selected *Authorization code* as the authorization grant type. The authorization code is obtained by using the authorization server – that you are configuring right now – as an intermediary between the client – the developer portal – and *backend-app* that you created previously. The client directs the *backend-app* then to the authorization server, which in turn directs the *backend-app* back to the client with an authorization code. The authorization endpoint URL-field is for the *OAuth 2.0 authorization endpoint (v2)* that you copied into your favorite text editor together with the *OAuth 2.0 token endpoint (v2)*; paste the second value (token) into the *Token endpoint URL*-field.

As the default scope, you set the Authorization scope of your *backend-app* from Figure 15-5. This value will be part of the JWT token which is included in an API request.

As the last step in Figure 15-11 for configuring the OAuth2 service, take the application ID of the *client-app* from Figure 15-7 and the client secret from Figure 15-8 and set both values accordingly.

Your OAuth 2.0 service is now configured. However, you are not done yet. Copy the *Authorization code grant flow* URL; you will need it in the next step where we head back to your client-app.

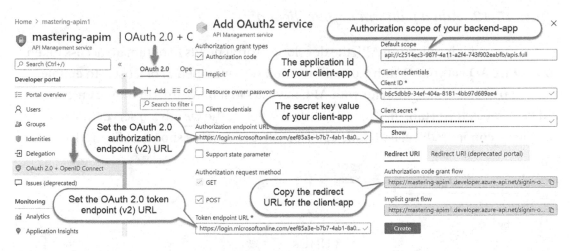

***Figure 15-11.** Configuring an OAuth 2.0 service*

Finally, you set a callback URL in your client-app that you copied in the previous step of Figure 15-10. The *Authorization code grant flow* URL is called after a user is successfully signed in.

Navigate back to your client-app in Azure AD and select *Authentication* from the left-hand menu and click **Add a platform** to add the *Authorization code grant flow* redirect URL; then click *Configure* as shown in Figure 15-12.

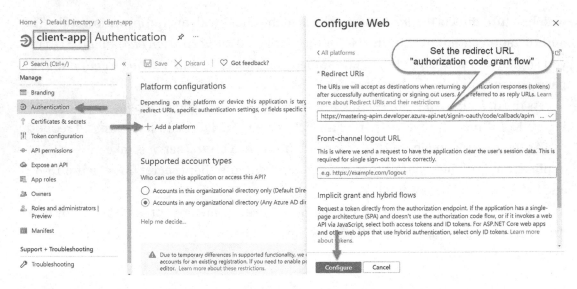

Figure 15-12. *Add a platform in your client-app*

Before making calls to an API, the developer portal needs to obtain an access token from Azure AD via your OAuth 2.0 authorization server on behalf of a user. To enable OAuth 2.0 user authorization for your API, navigate to it in Azure API Management and click the *Settings* tab; then select *OAuth 2.0*. Select the OAuth 2.0 server that you previously configured; I called mine `apim-oauth-service`, as shown in Figure 15-13.

Figure 15-13. *Setting OAuth 2.0 server for an API*

If you have not tried out the developer portal before, make sure to enable Cross-Origin-Resource-Sharing (CORS) for the developer portal by adding the following code to the global policy in Azure API Management. It permits loading resources also from other origins than its own, in this case `https://mastering-apim.developer.azure-api.net`.

```
<inbound>
    <cors allow-credentials="true">
        <allowed-origins>
        <origin>https://mastering-apim.developer.azure-api.net</origin>
    </allowed-origins>
    <allowed-methods preflight-result-max-age="300">
        <method>*</method>
    </allowed-methods>
    <allowed-headers>
        <header>*</header>
    </allowed-headers>
    <expose-headers>
        <header>*</header>
    </expose-headers>
    </cors>
</inbound>
```

Test and Validate

Before we take the last and final step in this section about authentication with OAuth 2.0, I want you to test the API that you enable OAuth 2.0 for from the developer portal. Navigate to the developer portal and try out an API endpoint; in this example, I selected the *GetTopics* endpoint of the *Demo Conference API,* as shown in Figure 15-14. On the right-hand side, you select `authorization_code` for the authorization method. A Microsoft sign-in window appears where you must provide your user credentials. After successful sign-in, an authorization header is added to the request, with a base64 encoded access token from Azure AD.

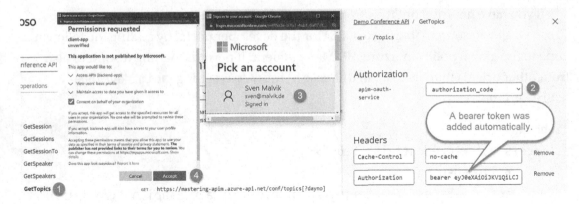

Figure 15-14. *Testing an OAuth 2.0–enabled API*

I mentioned briefly that an access token is a base64 encoded Json Web Token (JWT). If you are not familiar with JWTs or want to learn about it, please visit `https://jwt.io/` for a detailed documentation. In a nutshell, JWTs are credentials which can grant access to resources. They consist of three parts, header, payload, and signature, and have the following format: `HEADER.PAYLOAD.SIGNATURE`. The first part, the header, contains information about the algorithm and token type being used; the third and last part, the signature, which is used for verifying the integrity of the token and to verify that the sender of the JWT is who it says it is. Let's discuss the second part, the payload, in more detail.

The payload contains claims. They are statements about an entity such as a user and some additional data. In the example of Listing 15-4, I want to demonstrate to you the payload of my user that is signed in and authorized against the *Demo Conference API*.

Listing 15-4. JWT payload example

```
{
    "aud": "c2514ec3-987f-4a11-a2f4-743f902eabfb",
    "azp": "b6c5dbb9-34ef-404a-8181-4bb97d689ae4",
    "name": "Sven Malvik",
    "preferred_username": "sven@malvik.de",
    "oid": "810b562a-e63b-4603-a999-758e550506c1",
    "scp": "apis.full"
}
```

This payload shows not a complete list of all claims but a list of important claims to use in API policies for validating requests.

- **aud** represents the application ID of your backend-app.

- **azp** represents the application ID of your client-app.

- **name** represents the signed-in user.

- **preferred_username** represents the username for signing in user.

- **oid** represents the object ID of the user being signed in.

- **scp** represents the name of the scope of your backend-app.

You might ask yourself why you would want to validate access tokens in a request at all. What if a client calls an API with an invalid access token or without an access token at all? If a request does not have an authorization header, the call would still go through because there is nothing in Azure API Management that validates an access token by default. An authorization header with an access token would simply be passed through Azure API Management to the backend web service and nothing would prevent such invalid and eventual insecure requests from reaching the backend.

This is where API policies come in. You can pre-authorize requests in Azure API Management with the `Validate JWT` policy by validating the access tokens of each request. If a request does not have a valid access token and claims, your policy can simply block the request.

Your inbound policy requires an *Open ID Connect Discovery* endpoint, which is defined in an `openid-config` element; usually this endpoint has the following format: `https://login.microsoftonline.com/<APIM_SERVICE_NAME>.onmicrosoft.com/v2.0/.well-known/openid-configuration`. API Management will browse this endpoint when evaluating the policy, including the URLs which are in the response that are used to validate incoming JWTs. As you can see in Listing 15-5, I defined a `required-claim` element inside `openid-config` where I specified one claim, `aud` for audience. If the claim does not match the value defined in the policy, an error message is returned saying that the access token is invalid.

Listing 15-5. API policy for validating JWTs

```
<inbound>
    <base />
    <validate-jwt header-name="Authorization" failed-validation-
    httpcode="401" failed-validation-error-message="Unauthorized. Access
    token is missing or invalid.">
        <openid-config url="https://login.microsoftonline.com/svenmalvik.
        onmicrosoft.com/v2.0/.well-known/openid-configuration" />
        <required-claims>
            <claim name="aud">
                <value>c2514ec3-987f-4a11-a2f4-743f902eabfb</value>
            </claim>
        </required-claims>
    </validate-jwt>
    <set-backend-service base-url="https://conferenceapi.
    azurewebsites.net" />
</inbound>
```

Caution   Policies are great for pre-authorizing requests. However, backend web services should have their own implementation of access token validation as requests might come from other sources than your Azure API Management instance.

Depending on your use case, you can add more claims that you can verify against an access token.

Other Security Aspects

In this section, you will learn about some important security aspects of Azure API Management. You might already be familiar with some of them. However, I want to give you some more details that might not be known to you yet. Furthermore, you will learn about one security aspect you should implement in your global policy that you have not read about in this book.

Subscriptions

Subscriptions offer a way to secure access to APIs using subscription keys. API consumers that are in possession of a subscription key that is tied to a certain product or API may not be able to access other products and APIs, at least not by using the same subscription key. However, I see subscriptions more as a first line of defense, not as security per se, as subscription keys do not tell anything about what backend web service a client shall have access to. Neither do subscription keys identify users, just clients that might be represented by a group of users.

A second line of defense where you obtain an API consumer's identity itself is an excellent way of building an even more secure API layer. As requests may go other ways than via Azure API Management, I recommend implementing a way to authorize a client using JWTs. However, never rely on an external service only, such as your Azure API Management instance, when it comes to security. Instead, rely on your own security mechanism within your backend web services themselves, as requests may come from other sources than Azure API Management as well. Figure 15-15 illustrates the four lines of defense you might consider using.

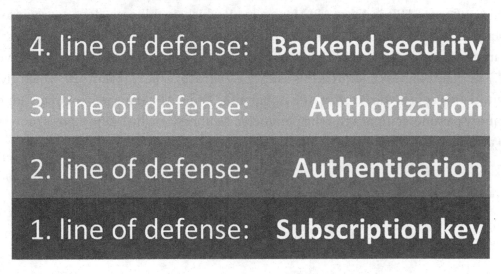

Figure 15-15. *Lines of defense*

Subscription keys offer a way to control API access for your customers. However, they are not a security barrier against cyberattacks. In that regard, I strongly recommend adding multiple layers of defense such as JWTs.

Protecting Against Path Traversal Attacks

A path traversal attack aims to access files and directories that are stored outside the web root folder. In case of web services such as API backend web services, it would mean that an API attacker accesses a web service it has access to with a manipulated request query parameter to gain access to a web service it has no access to. In other words, an API attacker exploits the path traversal vulnerability.

Imagine an attacker accessing a public API endpoint like `/conf/speaker/{id}`. Instead of setting a valid parameter such as the integer 1, the attacker uses the URL encoded path traversal string of `/../../petstore/pet/inventory`. The URL encoded version of this path would be `/conf/speaker%2f..%2f..%2fpetstore%2fpet%2finventory` where `%2f` is the URL encoded character of `/`.

Figure 15-16 illustrates such a path traversal attack where an attacker has access to the *Demo Conference API* via Azure API Management which, in this case, does not require a subscription key, it is publicly available. The *GetSession* operation of this API requires the `id` parameter which the attacker replaces with `%2f..%2f..%2fpetstore%2fpet%2finventory`. The Nginx ingress interprets this as `/../../petstore/pet/inventory`, which gives the attacker access to the *Pet store API*. Apparently, Azure API Management treats almost any query parameter input as a valid parameter. Neither does the Nginx ingress prevent such an attack from happening as illustrated in this example.

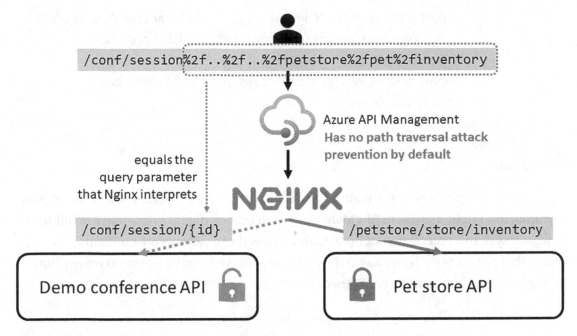

Figure 15-16. *Path traversal attack*

There are at least two options to protect backend web services from path traversal attacks:

1. Use Azure Application Gateway in front of Azure API Management with Web Application Firewall (WAF) enabled.

2. Block requests that include double dots, .., or %2e.

Listing 15-6 shows a global inbound policy that returns the status code *400* if the path of a request contains either .. or %2e%2e.

Listing 15-6. Global inbound policy for path traversal attack protection

```
<inbound>
    <choose>
        <when condition="@(context.Request.OriginalUrl.Path.Contains("..")
        || context.Request.OriginalUrl.Path.Contains("%2e%2e"))">
            <return-response>
                <set-status code="400" reason="Bad Request" />
```

```
                <set-header name="Content-Type" exists-action="override">
                    <value>application/json;charset=UTF-8</value>
                </set-header>
                <set-body>{"message": "Access denied."}</set-body>
            </return-response>
        </when>
    </choose>
</inbound>
```

A correct configured Nginx ingress will block path traversal attacks. However, as your organization might use Azure API Management to unlock digital assets that are hidden in legacy systems, you might not be sure about how these systems are configured. A policy that prevents such an attack will protect any of your digital assets no matter how an ingress or proxy might be configured.

Summary

This chapter focused on security aspects of Azure API Management that you have not learned about in previous chapters, such as HTTP basic authentication and OAuth 2.0. Furthermore, you learned why and how you can use Azure API Management policies to prevent path traversal attacks. Lastly, you learned that subscription keys are not enough as the only security barrier and what other lines of defense you should implement.

CHAPTER 16

Logging and Monitoring

Until now, you have sent requests to APIs in Azure API Management and then received a response. Hopefully you were lucky, and all requests were successfully right from the beginning. However, as luck is not a concept we can rely on, we need to know exactly what happens with our requests. This is not only true for failing requests but also for those that were successful and return HTTP code 200 (OK), as you might have non-functional requirements such as tight response times that you must verify.

You might already have noticed in the Azure portal for Azure API Management that you get tracing information when you send a test request. The HTTP response shows two parts, *Message* and **Trace**. The tracing information shows an API inspector for all policy sections with detailed information, as Figure 16-1 shows.

Figure 16-1. *Tracing information for an API request*

To get the same tracing information when sending a request with cURL or Postman, you must add the `Ocp-Apim-Trace` header to a request and set the value to `true`. The response will contain the `Ocp-Apim-Trace-Location` header with an Azure Storage Account blob location where you find the same tracing information.

In this chapter, you will first learn how to log custom data to an Azure Event Hub that other services can consume. You will then learn about Azure Log Analytics which provides you with insights ranging from timeline to requests and how you can run predefined and custom *Kusto* queries on all the available telemetry that Azure API

© Sven Malvik 2022

S. Malvik, *Mastering Azure API Management*, https://doi.org/10.1007/978-1-4842-8011-9_16

Management generates. Lastly, you will create an Azure Application Insights resource to analyze requests for anomalies.

Logging via Event Hub

Logging from Azure API Management to Azure Event Hub is useful for several reasons. Logs can be consumed by other services, they can be analyzed with Azure Stream Analytics, and they can be useful when developing Azure API Management policies. I use them often to "debug" policies I develop in conjunction with VS Code as this section will demonstrate.

In this section, you will log data from the Demo Conference API in Azure API Management as events to Azure Event Hub, as Figure 16-2 illustrates. From there, events can be consumed by other systems and services, such as Splunk, Azure Stream Analytics, or others.

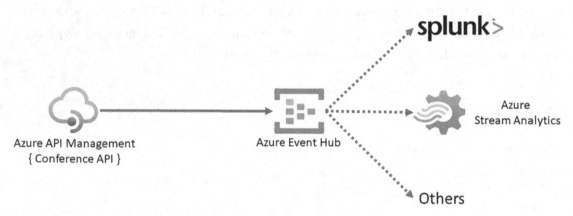

Figure 16-2. *Streaming logs to Azure Event Hub*

Azure Event Hubs is an event ingestion service and data streaming platform managed by Microsoft Azure. You can read more about Azure Event Hub on Microsoft's official documentation.

As always, when you work with Azure PowerShell toward an Azure API Management instance, you must set the right context, in this case for *mastering-apim,* as Listing 16-1 shows.

Listing 16-1. Set the context for your Azure API Management instance

```
# Get subscription
$context = Get-AzSubscription -SubscriptionId <SUBSCRIPTION_ID>

# Set subscription by setting the context
Set-AzContext $context

# Set context for Azure API Management instance
$apimContext = New-AzApiManagementContext `
        -ResourceGroupName mastering-apim-rg `
        -ServiceName mastering-apim
```

Deploy an Azure Event Hub

If you are already familiar with Azure Event Hubs, you know that you need a namespace to scope events in a container. Create a namespace in the same resource group as your Azure API Management instance and name it `mastering-apim-eh-ns`.

As Listing 16-2 shows, I chose the basic pricing tier `SkuName` with the lowest capacity `SkuCapacity` for the event hub throughput, which works fine for this example. In a production environment, you might consider the standard or premium tier which gives you longer event retention and more features.

Listing 16-2. Create a new Event Hub namespace

```
# Create Event Hub namespace
New-AzEventHubNamespace `
        -ResourceGroupName "mastering-apim-rg" `
        -Name "mastering-apim-eh-ns" `
        -Location "West Europe" `
        -SkuName "Basic" `
        -SkuCapacity 1
```

The next step is to create an Azure Event Hub for those events that come from Azure API Management. Use the Azure PowerShell cmdlet `New-AzEventHub`, as Listing 16-3 shows, and give it the name *mastering-apim-eh*.

Listing 16-3. Deploy an Azure Event Hub

```
# Create Event Hub
New-AzEventHub `
        -ResourceGroupName "mastering-apim-rg" `
        -NamespaceName "mastering-apim-eh-ns" `
        -Name "mastering-apim-eh"
```

You have now deployed an Azure Event Hub that you can use to send logs to from your Azure API Management instance.

Set Event Hub Logger to Azure API Management

The Azure PowerShell module is a great way to automate infrastructure across environments. Alternatively, you can create an Azure Event Hub namespace and an Event Hub manually from the Azure portal. This is not the case for the Event Hub logger that Azure API Management needs to log to your Azure Event Hub. Here, you must use either the Azure REST API or Azure PowerShell.

To create a logger in Azure API Management for an Azure Event Hub, you need a connection string from your Event Hub, which is configured with one or more authorization rules, *listen*, *send*, and *manage*.

Listing 16-4 shows how to create an authorization rule for your specific Event Hub namespace *mastering-apim-eh-ns* using the Azure PowerShell cmdlet New-AzEventHubAuthorizationRule. I set Rights to *listen* and *send* as Azure API Management does not need to manage the namespace.

Listing 16-4. Add EventHub logger

```
# Add Access to Event Hubs namespace
New-AzEventHubAuthorizationRule `
        -ResourceGroupName "mastering-apim-rg" `
        -NamespaceName "mastering-apim-eh-ns" `
        -AuthorizationRuleName "mastering-apim-eh-auth-rule" `
        -Rights @("Listen", "Send")
```

Use `Get-AzEventHubKey` to read either the primary or secondary connection string for your Event Hub and store the value in a variable $ehConnection, as Listing 16-5 shows. Set the authorization rule *mastering-apim-eh-auth-rule* of Listing 16-4 for the parameter `AuthorizationRuleName`.

Listing 16-5.   Set the connection string for the Event Hub

```
# Get the connectionString to the Event Hubs namespace
$ehConnection = (Get-AzEventHubKey `
        -ResourceGroupName "mastering-apim-rg" `
        -NamespaceName "mastering-apim-eh-ns" `
        -AuthorizationRuleName "mastering-apim-eh-auth-rule")
        .PrimaryConnectionString
```

Now that you have a valid connection string for your Event Hub, you can create the Azure API Management logger by using the Azure PowerShell cmdlet `New-AzApiManagementLogger`. Set the connections string for the `ConnectionString` parameter by concatenating your connection string $ehConnection with `;EntityPath=mastering-apim-eh`, as Listing 16-6 shows. The entity path is the name of your Event Hub.

Listing 16-6.   Create Event Hub logger

```
# Create Azure API Management Event Hub logger
New-AzApiManagementLogger `
        -Context $apimCtx `
        -LoggerId "mastering-apim-logger" `
        -Name "mastering-apim-logger" `
        -ConnectionString "$ehConnection;EntityPath=mastering-apim-eh"
```

It is a good practice to set a name – in this case, *mastering-apim-logger* – shown in Listing 16-6, so you do not get a generated name which might be hard to know the purpose of in the future.

Add Event Hub Logger to Policy

You can create multiple loggers in Azure API Management and use them in different scenarios or for different products, APIs, and operations. In the example in Listing 16-7, you add the logger `mastering-apim-logger` to the *Demo Conference API* policy by using the `log-to-eventhub` policy. The value is a concatenated string containing DateTime, service name, RequestId, IP address, and the operation name. You can also log a JSON string or other strings in other formats.

Listing 16-7. Policy for Event Hub logger

```
<inbound>
        <!-- Create API policy and add Event Hub logger to API -->
        <log-to-eventhub logger-id ='mastering-apim-logger'>
    @( string.Join(",", DateTime.UtcNow, context.Deployment.ServiceName,
    context.RequestId, context.Request.IpAddress, context.Operation.Name) )
        </log-to-eventhub>
</inbound>
```

All incoming requests will now log to the Azure Event Hub `mastering-apim-eh` and can be consumed by other services.

Observing Logs with VS Code

After logging in to your Event Hub, you might ask yourself, how you can see the logs. The answer is by using the VS Code extension *Azure Event Hub Explorer*. Figure 16-3 demonstrates how to find the extension and then install it.

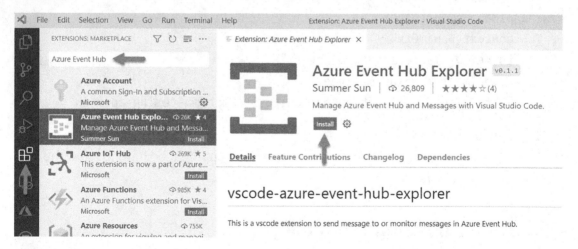

Figure 16-3. *Install VC Code extension Azure Event Hub Explorer*

To observe your requests in VS Code, you need to configure the extension by selecting your Azure Event Hub. Start the configuration process by choosing **Select Event Hub** (shown in Figure 16-4) and follow the steps which will navigate you to set your Even Hub `mastering-apim-eh`. You get asked to sign in to your Azure account, select your subscription, Event Hub namespace, and finally your Event Hub.

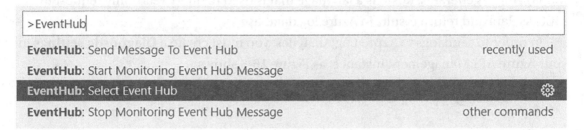

Figure 16-4. *Set Event Hub in VS Code*

After you have successfully set your Event Hub, select **Start Monitoring Event Hub Message** to start observing incoming events.

Listing 16-8 shows an example of how the extension prints log messages. As you can see, it prints the date and time, service name, request id, IP address, and the name of the operation that I called.

Listing 16-8. Log messages from the Azure Event Hub Explorer extension

```
Azure Event Hub Explorer > Start monitoring event hub
Azure Event Hub Explorer > Created partition receiver [1] for consumerGroup
[$Default]
Azure Event Hub Explorer > Created partition receiver [0] for consumerGroup
[$Default]
Azure Event Hub Explorer > Message Received:
"4/8/2020 5:33:09 PM,mastering-apim.azure-api.net,00a166ad-beb4-4b1a-bc56-
8faf699eca6e,51.175.196.188,GetTopics"
Azure Event Hub Explorer > Stop monitoring event hub
```

Congratulations if you have successfully followed all steps. You can stop observing your Event Hub by selecting **Stop Monitoring Event Hub Message**.

Logging to Azure Log Analytics

A ready-to-use monitor capability of Azure API Management is Log Analytics. Azure Log Analytics provides you with insights ranging from timeline to requests where you can run predefined and custom *Kusto* queries on all the available telemetry that Azure API Management generates. Kusto is a language that is used to query read-only request to process data and return results in Azure log databases.

In order to send logs to Azure Log Analytics, you must create a **Diagnostic settings** in your Azure API Management instance, as Figure 16-5 shows.

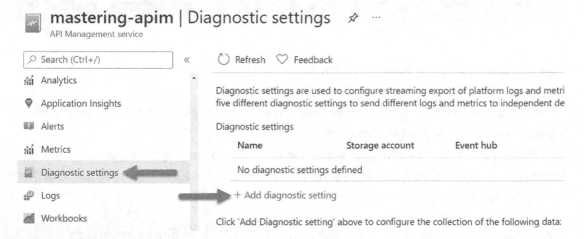

Figure 16-5. *Add diagnostic settings*

In the following example, I selected *GatewayLogs* to send those logs to a Log Analytics workspace, as Figure 16-6 shows. Select **Resource specific** as the destination table where data is written to individual tables for each category of the resource instead of one *AzureDiagnostic* table.

Diagnostic setting ···

🖫 Save   ✕ Discard   🗑 Delete   ♡ Feedback

A diagnostic setting specifies a list of categories of platform logs and/or metrics that you want to collect from a resource, and one or more destinations that you would stream them to. Normal usage charges for the destination will occur. Learn more about the different log categories and contents of those logs

Diagnostic setting name * | gwlogs   ✓ |

Category details   Destination details

log   ☑ Send to Log Analytics workspace

☑ GatewayLogs   Subscription
                                              | Visual Studio Enterprise Subscription   ∨ |

☐ WebSocketConnectionLogs   Log Analytics workspace
                                              | DefaultWorkspace-b0e68700-2b10-4f92-858a-36d2a98748b8-WEU (West... ∨ |
metric
                                              Destination table ⓘ
☐ AllMetrics   (Azure diagnostics)(**Resource specific**) ⬅

Figure 16-6. Configuring diagnostic settings

All traffic that goes through an API gateway is now logged to your Azure Log Analytics workspace. Send a few requests with cURL from your local terminal or the Developer portal of your Azure API Management instance and click Analytics in the left-hand menu.

Analytics shows these calls in a timeline, as Figure 16-7 shows, where nine calls succeeded and two calls failed; I forgot to set the subscription key for those failed requests.

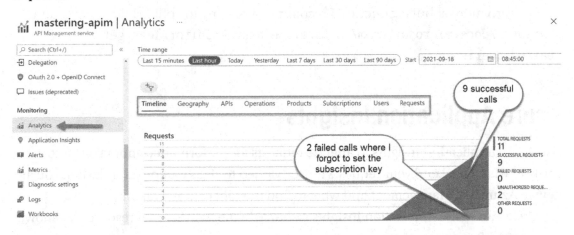

Figure 16-7. Incoming traffic

There is more information that might be useful and that are more specific depending on your use case. You can click through the other tabs such as APIs, Products, or Users.

A programmatic way of retrieving gateway logs is by using KQL (Kusto query language) in Log Analytics where you use queries. Log Analytics provides a set of predefined queries such as *Number of requests, Last 100 failed requests,* or *Overall latency.*

Figure 16-8 shows an example query with KQL for reading the number of requests.

Figure 16-8. *A simple Kusto query in Azure Log Analytics*

To learn more about log queries, I recommend reading the official documentation at https://docs.microsoft.com/en-us/azure/azure-monitor/logs/get-started-queries.

Azure Application Insights

Use Azure Application Insights to analyze requests for performance anomalies or to verify to which backend your requests are forwarded to. This is very helpful when you are new to Azure API Management and what to find the root cause of an error.

Create an Azure Application Insights resource in the Azure portal resource, as shown in Figure 16-9. Set your Azure subscription, resource group, and a name. As the resource mode, select *Workspace-based,* as *Classic* is deprecated. If you have not created a **Log Analytics Workspace** earlier, Azure will automatically create one. In my case, Azure created a *Log Analytics Workspace* in the region *West US* which is not my preferred

region, so I created a *Log Analytics Workspace* resource separately in the Azure portal
and selected that one instead.

Application Insights   ...

Monitor web app performance and usage

Select a subscription to manage deployed resources and costs. Use resource groups like folders to organize and manage all
your resources.

Subscription * ⓘ	Visual Studio Enterprise Subscription ⌄
└─── Resource Group * ⓘ	mastering-apim-rg ⌄
	Create new

INSTANCE DETAILS

Name * ⓘ	mastering-apim-appinsights ✓
Region * ⓘ	(Europe) West Europe ⌄
Resource Mode * ⓘ	Classic **Workspace-based**

WORKSPACE DETAILS

Subscription * ⓘ	Visual Studio Enterprise Subscription ⌄
└─── *Log Analytics Workspace ⓘ	DefaultWorkspace-b0e68700-2b10-4f92-858a-36d2a98748b8-WEU [West... ⌄

Figure 16-9. *Create Azure Application Insights resource in Azure portal*

Navigate to your Azure API Management instance and choose *Application Insight*
from the left-hand menu and click **Add** to select your Azure Application Insights
resource. As Figure 16-10 shows, I added my newly created Application Insights resource
`mastering-apim-appinsights`.

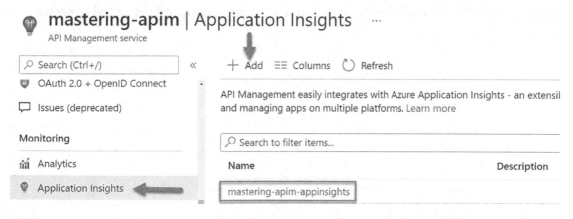

Figure 16-10. *Adding Application Insights to Azure API Management*

Requests are not automatically logged to Application Insights. Instead, you must enable Application Insights for your APIs first. Figure 16-11 shows how to enable Application Insights for an individual API. Click *All APIs* to set this globally. There is one very important setting, *Sampling*. It is a value between 0 and 100% and determines how much you want to log.

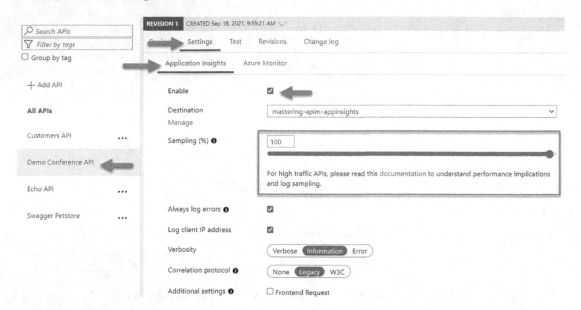

Figure 16-11. *Enabling Application Insights for an API*

Send a few requests to one of the APIs for which you enabled Application Insights and navigate to this Application Insights resource.

Figure 16-12 shows the *Transaction search* where all requests are listed. Click on one request to get details such as response time, called operation, and the called backend service.

Figure 16-12. *Transaction search in Application Insights*

Warning   Logging all events has serious performance implications. Based on internal load tests from Microsoft, logging to Application Insights caused a 40%–50% reduction in throughput when request rate exceeded 1000 requests per second.

A good compromise in a production environment is to log from Azure API Management to Application Insights only if there is a strong need as in an ongoing incident where you need to rely on as much information as possible. When it comes to the test environment where performance is not always an issue, you might want to set the sampling rate to 100%, so developers have all necessary information to build great APIs.

Summary

In this chapter, you learned how to log custom data but also how to monitor API traffic. When logging to Azure Event Hub through policies rather than using diagnostic settings with Azure Event Hub as destination, you have the advantage of logging custom data. However, when logging custom data to Azure Event Hub, be careful and do not put too much logic into policies. Policies in Azure API Management can be expensive as they are often hard shared across multiple teams and therefore hard to maintain; this is especially true for product policies and the global policy. If you do not need to log custom data, I recommend enabling diagnostic settings with Azure Event Hub, at least in your test environment. For the production environment, you must be aware of a decrease in performance. That is also the reason why you can set a sample rate from 0% to 100% logging.

## CHAPTER 17

Administration

In this chapter, you will learn about Azure API Management's capabilities of high availability by scaling it and deploying API gateways to multiple regions. Furthermore, you will learn to prepare your Azure API Management instance for an event of a disaster by taking backups that can be restored in another instance of Azure API Management. As high availability often comes together with the non-functional requirement of great performance, caching might be a preferable and suitable solution. Azure API Management has, for that reason, a built-in cache which does not necessarily work together with high availability. You will learn why this is the case and how to configure an external cache for your Azure API Management instance.

Until this chapter, you, as an API consumer, have accessed Azure API Management by using the default domain `<SERVICE_NAME>.azure-api.net`. As this is not always a preferred domain, you will learn how to configure a custom domain with TLS/SSL.

I will also teach you to generate API usage reports. These are especially important when you want to monetize your APIs, but also to find out what digital assets are accessed the most.

Furthermore, you learn to use Azure Automation to make changes in your Azure API Management instance in an automatic way. This is very useful when working with repetitive tasks such as taking backups.

Finally, you will learn how to combine multiple Azure Logic Apps into one API and why you would want this.

High Availability

High availability can be achieved by using several different features in Azure API Management such as scaling your instance depending on traffic volume, failover all traffic to another region in case of a regional outage, and taking backups that can be restored in another instance when necessary.

In this section, you will first learn to scale your Azure API Management instance based on the *Capacity* metric. We will then discuss multi-region deployments and availability zones for the managed API gateway. Furthermore, you will learn to take a backup of an instance and restore it in another instance.

Scaling in Regions

When you deploy Azure API Management with the *Consumption* pricing tier, you do not need to worry about high traffic volume as your instance automatically scales. This is not true for all the other pricing tiers, especially not the *Developer* pricing tier, which can't be scaled; its default is one *unit*.

A *unit* has no fixed number of requests that it can handle as this depends on the size of the requests, all involved policies, the system operations such as TLS handshakes on new connections that are executed, but also the load on the developer portal. To determine whether you need to scale up to serve an increased amount of traffic volume or to scale down to save costs in low traffic volume times, you use the **Capacity** metric.

Figure 17-1 shows the capacity of the Azure API Management instance that I use in this book for the last 30 days.

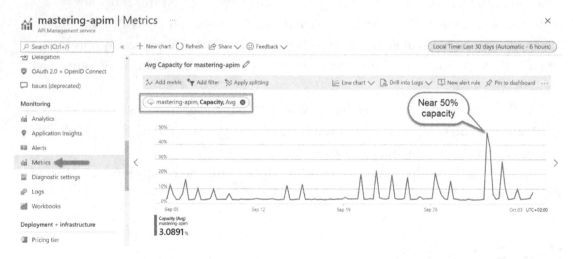

Figure 17-1. *Capacity metric in Azure API Management*

The capacity reached almost 50% on the 30th of September. In preparation of a Black-Friday event where you eventually expect high volume traffic, you might want to increase the number of units the day before as the scaling process takes at least 20 minutes up to 45 minutes.

One option to scale the number of units is from within the Azure portal. Figure 17-2 shows how to change the number of units in Azure API Management by clicking **Locations** in the left-hand menu and selecting your region.

Figure 17-2. *Scaling Azure API Management*

In this example, I have Azure API Management instance deployed in one region only, *West Europe*. API consumers that send requests from other parts of the world would naturally experience higher latency and the API experience would suffer. Luckily, you can add additional, secondary regions that are closer to those API consumers. However, secondary regions have only the managed API gateway deployed, not the developer portal or service management component.

In case the primary region is inaccessible, all API consumers will be routed to the closest secondary location unless you already use an Azure service such as Azure Traffic Manager that sends API consumers to the closest API gateway locations.

Be aware that requests are routed to the same backend web services as before. An incoming request in a secondary region *West US* will still forward the request to the primary region *West Europe* unless you change the global policy and set a different URL to a different backend as the following code demonstrates:

```
<inbound>
    <base />
    <choose>
        <when condition="@("West US".Equals(context.Deployment.Region,
        StringComparison.OrdinalIgnoreCase))">
```

```
            <set-backend-service base-url="<WEST_US_URL>" />
        </when>
        <otherwise>
            <set-backend-service base-url="WEST_EUROPE_URL" />
        </otherwise>
    </choose>
</inbound>
```

Another option to achieve high availability of your APIs is by enabling zone redundancy using *Availability zones*.

Note   Availability zones and multi-region deployments are only available in the Premium and Standard pricing tiers of Azure API Management.

Availability Zones are unique physical locations within an Azure region. It protects your APIs in case of a failure within the data center your Azure API Management instance is deployed to. For high availability, it makes sense to deploy your instance to at least two availability zones, as Figure 17-2 shows.

Preparing for a Disaster with Backup and Restore

Hopefully, a serious disaster to the region where your Azure API Management instance is located, and where all your data such as APIs, users, and subscriptions are deployed to, will never occur. However, it is a possibility that you might want to prepare for. One option to prepare for such an unlikely event of a disaster where you must recover fast in separate Azure API Management instance is by taking regular backups of your primary Azure API Management instance and restore the latest backup, if necessary, in the secondary, target instance.

In a project I worked in, we had another use case where we emphasized immutable infrastructure. We wanted to reduce the risk of potential traffic failures due to changes in the infrastructure. Instead of upgrading central infrastructure components such as Azure Kubernetes Service or routing certain traffic through a new Azure Application Gateway, we deployed a new infrastructure cluster with all its components and changes before we tested everything there. This includes Azure API Management. Taking backups from the active Azure API Management instance and then restoring the backup in the new instance was part of it.

In this section, you will learn how to take a backup from your primary Azure API Management instance and restore it in your secondary instance, so everything works as before. You might already have a primary instance of Azure API Management with some APIs, users, and subscriptions. Before you begin to take a backup from it, create a secondary instance with the same pricing tier.

Note   The *Consumption* pricing tier is not supported.

The following Azure PowerShell cmdlet `New-AzApiManagement` creates a new instance `mastering-apim-dest` in the *North Europe* region, as my primary instance is running in the *West Europe* region. If you do not define the `Sku` parameter, the instance will set it to the *Developer* tier.

```
New-AzApiManagement `
        -ResourceGroupName "mastering-apim-rg" `
        -Name "mastering-apim-dest" `
        -Location "North Europe" `
        -Organization "myOrg" `
        -AdminEmail "sven@malvik.de"
```

Create an Azure storage account and container close to the secondary Azure API Management instance in *North Europe* to store your Azure API Management backups, as the code example of Listing 17-1 shows.

Listing 17-1. Create Azure Storage for Azure API Management backups.

```
$storageAccount = New-AzStorageAccount `
        -ResourceGroupName "mastering-apim-rg" `
        -Name "masteringapimsa" `
        -SkuName Standard_LRS `
        -Location "North Europe"

New-AzStorageContainer `
        -Name "mastering-apim-backups" `
        -Context $storageAccount.Context `
        -Permission blob
```

To take a backup of your Azure API Management instance `mastering-apim`, use the Azure PowerShell cmdlet `Backup-AzApiManagement`. The cmdlet requires the storage account for the `StorageContext` parameter and the name of the container for the `TargetContainerName` parameter. You created both in Listing 17-1. Choose then a name of your backup and set it for the `TargetBlobName` parameter; mine is `mastering-apim-backup`, but you might consider appending a timestamp to the name as you ideally will take daily backups using an Azure Automation account.

```
Backup-AzApiManagement `
        -ResourceGroupName "mastering-apim-rg" `
        -Name "mastering-apim" `
        -StorageContext $storageAccount.Context `
        -TargetContainerName "mastering-apim-backups" `
        -TargetBlobName "mastering-apim-backup"
```

The complementary cmdlet to a backup operation is `Restore-AzApiManagement`. It requires almost the same parameters. Instead of target parameters, it expects source parameters for the storage account of the backup.

```
Restore-AzApiManagement `
        -ResourceGroupName "mastering-apim-rg" `
        -Name "mastering-apim-dest" `
        -StorageContext $storageAccount.Context `
        -SourceContainerName "mastering-apim-backups" `
        -SourceBlobName "mastering-apim-src-backup"
```

Restoring a backup will not change any values that are specific to the secondary target Azure API Management instance. Keep both instances as alike as possible, so you avoid doing as few post operations as possible.

Doing a backup/restore operation can take some time depending on the number of APIs, users, subscriptions, etc., that you have deployed. In some cases where we wanted to switch all traffic to the new infrastructure cluster, the restore operation hung. It became such a problem for us that we excluded Azure API Management from the list of Azure components to be redeployed to the new infrastructure cluster, so we were not dependent on it anymore. Still, we take regular backups, so we are prepared for an eventual disaster.

Configuring External Caching

Caching is a way of speeding up your web service performance. Instead of forwarding *all* requests to backend web services and waiting for the responses, responses that are not expected to change over a specific time interval might be candidates for storing in a data store with fast read access and that is closer to the API gateway. Azure API Management provides therefore an internal cache where you control the data that goes into the cache by using the `cache-lookup` policy.

Figure 17-3 demonstrates a basic example of a caching policy. Responses are cached by the two headers, `Accept` and `Accept-Charset`. Requests with matching headers will have the cached response returned, until the cache duration interval of ten seconds has expired using the `cache-store` policy. Both, `cache-lookup` in the inbound section and `cache-store` in the outbound section go hand in hand and must be defined together.

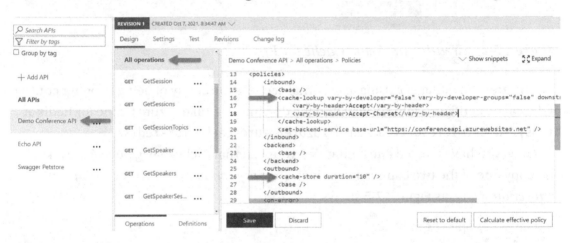

Figure 17-3. *Simple caching policy*

Note   The internal cache is not available in the *Consumption* pricing tier. Instead, use an external cache.

An external cache is not only a must when using the Consumption pricing tier but also when your Azure API Management instance supports multiple regions as the internal cache uses a shared per-tenant data cache. As you scale up to multiple units, you get access to the cached data within the same region. Caching across regions depends on an external cache such as Azure Cache for Redis.

Search for *Azure Cache for Redis* in the Azure portal and click **Create,** as Figure 17-4 shows.

Figure 17-4. *Creating an Azure Cache for Redis*

The great advantage of using an external cache is the ability of being in better control of the cache configuration. You can find the documentation of Azure Cache for Redis at `https://docs.microsoft.com/en-us/azure/azure-cache-for-redis/`.

Once you have created and configured your external cache, navigate to Access keys, and copy one of the two connection strings, *Primary connection string* or *Secondary connection string,* as Figure 17-5 shows.

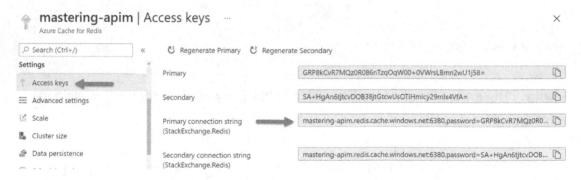

Figure 17-5. *Getting the connection string*

The connections string for the cache is required by your Azure API Management instance, so this external cache can be used instead of the internal cache.

Navigate to your Azure API Management instance and click **External cache** and **Add** your external cache. Figure 17-6 demonstrates how to add your Azure Cache for Redis resource as the external cache for the Azure API Management instance *mastering-apim* that is currently running in the *West Europe* region. Paste the connection string from Figure 17-5 into the corresponding field and click **Save**.

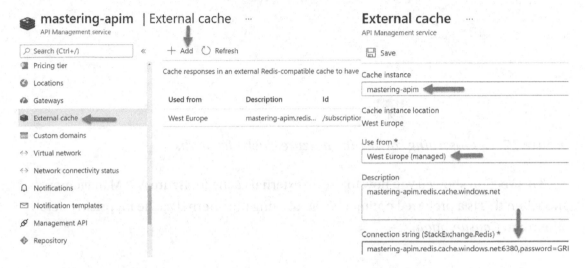

Figure 17-6. *Adding the external cache to Azure API Management*

To verify that responses are stored in this external cache, send a few requests to an API such as the *Demo Conference API* as shown in the following:

```
curl -i https://mastering-apim.azure-api.net/conf/topics
```

Navigate then to your external cache in the Azure portal and select *Metrics* where you filter for **Cache Hits** in the last 30 days. As you can see in Figure 17-7, I send several requests where 24 responses came from the external cache instead of the backend web service.

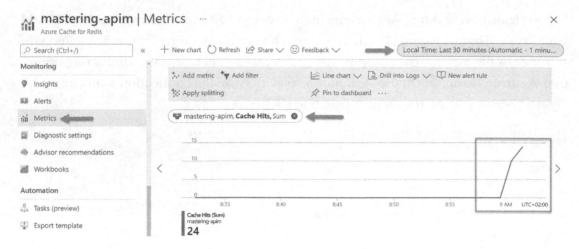

Figure 17-7. *Observing cache hits in Azure Cache for Redis*

This section showed you how to use an external cache for Azure API Management and when this is a preferred option instead of using the internal cache for pricing tiers other than *Consumption*.

Adding Custom Domains

To this chapter, API consumers used the default subdomains `<SERVICE_NAME>.azure-api.net` to access the API gateway and `<SERVICE_NAME>.developer.azure-api.net` to access the developer portal. You can change these subdomains and the subdomains for managing your Azure API Management instance and accessing SCM by configuring one or more custom domains. This might be useful regarding your corporate identity.

In this section, you will learn to set a custom domain for the developer portal. Instead of accessing the developer portal at `mastering-apim.developer.azure-api.net`, I will show you how to change this subdomain to another subdomain, in this example, to `dev.svenmalvik.com`.

A first step to achieve this is by creating a *CNAME* record on your DNS server. A CNAME record (alias record) maps one domain or subdomain to a canonical name. In the following example, the *alias* `dev.svenmalvik.com` maps to the *canonical name* `mastering-apim.developer.azure-api.net`.

Alias: `dev.svenmalvik.com`
Canonical name: `mastering-apim.developer.azure-api.net`

To enable your Azure API Management instance to securely expose URLs with HTTPS over TLS/SSL, you need a certificate where the subject matches the CNAME, in this case `dev.svenmalvik.com`. You can either bring your own certificate or create one in Azure Key Vault, either a self-signed certificate or one that is issued by a certificate authority. I recommend using Azure Key Vault, as certificates can be renewed automatically.

Figure 17-8 shows the Azure Key Vault *MasteringApimKeyVault* that you created in Chapter 7 (section "Secrets from Azure Key Vault"). Navigate to your Azure Key Vault and select *Certificates* from the left-hand menu and click **Generate/Import** to create a new certificate.

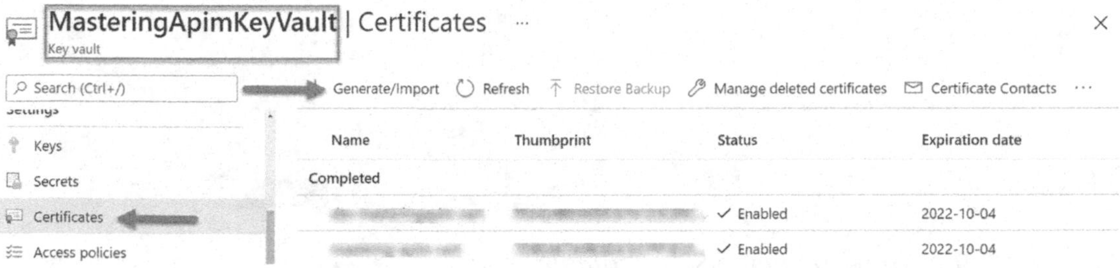

Figure 17-8. *Generate SSL certificate in Azure Key Vault*

If you have not created an Azure Key Vault yet, make sure to create one that Azure API Management can access by enabling managed system identity (MSI) in your instance. Give the new created principal ID the permissions *list* and *get* for certificates on this Azure Key Vault, so your Azure API Management instance can list and get your certificate.

In Figure 17-9, I created a **self-signed certificate**. In a production environment, you might consider creating one that is issued by a public certificate authority, so this certificate is automatically trusted by your clients. Alternatively, you can install your certificate at your clients. Set the **Subject** parameter to `CN=<YOUR_CNAME>`. I chose to automatically renew the certificate. The process of creating a certificate takes up to 15 minutes.

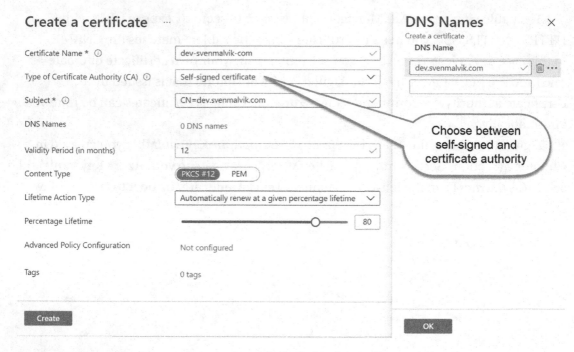

Figure 17-9.   Configure new SSL certificate

Navigate to your Azure API Management instance and select **Custom domains** from the left-hand menu; then click **Add** and set your CNAME in the **Hostname** field. Also select your certificate from your Azure Key Vault, as shown in Figure 17-10.

Figure 17-10.   Add new custom domain in Azure API Management

The result of custom domains for this exercise are shown in Figure 17-11. It shows the default domain and two custom domains that I created, `dev.svenmalvik.com` and `api.svenmalvik.com`.

Endpoint ↑↓	Hostname ↑↓	Certificate ↑↓	Nego...↑↓	D.↑↓	Certificate key vault id ↑↓	
Developer portal	dev.svenmalvik.com	Expiry: 2022-10-04, thumbprint: F6342...			https://masteringapimkeyvault.vault.az...	•••
Gateway	mastering-apim.azure-api.net					•••
Gateway	api.svenmalvik.com	Expiry: 2022-10-04, thumbprint: 7DBEA...		✓	https://masteringapimkeyvault.vault.az...	•••

Figure 17-11. *List of custom domains*

When you access the developer portal in your browser and navigate to your custom domain, you will probably get a warning *Not secure,* as you can see in Figure 17-12. This happens because you created a self-signed certificate that is not in the browsers list of trusted certificate authorities. You can solve this issue by either installing this certificate on all known clients such as your internal API consumers, or by issuing a certificate from a publicly trusted certificate authority.

Figure 17-12. *Accessing developer portal with custom domain*

Monetizing Your APIs with User Reports

Azure API Management is an ideal service to monetize your digital assets as it can provide you with detailed insights about the usage of products, APIs, operations, subscriptions, and more.

In the following example, you will retrieve user reports. As Azure API Management reports are currently not available through Azure PowerShell, you will use the REST API to retrieve reports from your API Management instance. The data that you retrieve is in JSON format.

Start by opening the Azure portal and navigating to your Azure API Management instance. Click **Management API** in the left-hand menu and enable the management REST API, as Figure 17-13 shows.

Figure 17-13. *Enabling the management REST API*

Switch to your Azure Cloud shell in *Bash* mode and set the following variables that identify your Azure API Management instance.

```
SERVICE="mastering-apim"
RESOURCE_GROUP="mastering-apim-rg"
SUBSCRIPTION_ID="YOUR_SUBSCRIPTION_ID"
```

To interact with your instance, set the subscription of where your Azure API Management instance is deployed to by using the Azure CLI and the `SUBSCRIPTION_ID` variable that you declared.

```
az account set -s $SUBSCRIPTION_ID$
```

Also, set the management URL for your Azure API Management instance. This is the base URL for managing your Azure API Management instance.

```
URL=https://$SERVICE.management.azure-api.net/subscriptions/$SUBSCRIPTION_
ID/resourceGroups/$RESOURCE_GROUP/providers/Microsoft.ApiManagement/
service/$SERVICE
```

The Azure API Management REST API provides several reports operations. The following example retrieves a report for all users /byUser. Other operations are /byApi, /byGeo, /byOperation, /byProduct, /byRequest, /bySubscription, and /byTime.

```
REPORT="/reports/byUser"
```

Nobody can access your reports yet as you have not authorized yourself with a Shared Access Signature (SAS) token. The simplest way of getting a SAS token is from the Azure portal, as Figure 17-14 shows.

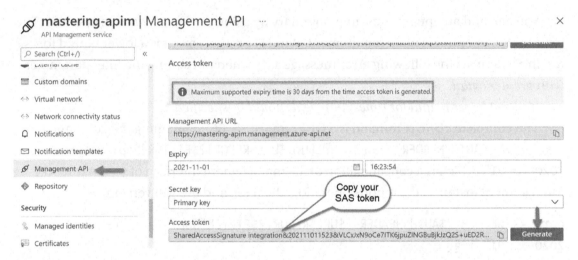

Figure 17-14. *Generating a SAS token*

Click Generate to create your SAS token and copy it. You authenticate yourself by setting an authentication header to every request using the SAS token. Create a new variable AUTH_HEADER in your Bash session and set your SAS token as the value, as shown in the following:

```
AUTH_HEADER="Authorization: <YOUR_SAS_TOKEN>"
```

Note   Your SAS token is valid for a maximum of 30 days before you must regenerate it.

You are almost done creating a request. As you can potentially get many data from your Azure API Management instance, all reports operations want to know from what date and time you are requesting data. You do this by setting a filter as a query parameter. The filter parameter is called `$filter` which means that you must escape the dollar character using `%24` instead. The same is true for other special characters such as spaces and tickers as the following example demonstrates:

```
$filter=timestamp ge datetime'2021-06-01T00:00:00' xx
```

The preceding filter defines a timeframe from a specific date and time until now using the operator *greater equal* `ge`.

```
FILTER="%24filter=timestamp%20ge%20datetime%272021-06-01T00:00:00%27"
```

You *can* add an upper timestamp boundary by using the *lower equal* `le` operator. The *lower equal* operator is not a requirement. What is a requirement is a lower bound for the timestamp as the following error message says when not setting the filter parameter with *greater equal*.

"At least lower bound for timestamp field should be specified."

The complete *cURL* command is a GET request `-X GET` containing the authentication header `-H "$AUTH_HEADER"`, and the full URL `$URL$REPORT?$FILTER"&api-version=2020-12-01"`, which is a concatenation of the management interface of your Azure API Management instance, the reports operation, the filter, and the API version.

```
curl -X GET -H "$AUTH_HEADER" $URL$REPORT?$FILTER"&api-version=
2020-12-01" | jq
```

I piped the response to `jq`, a popular JSON command-line processor that makes the JSON response more readable.

The following JSON object represents the user *Max Vax* of the response containing all users:

```
{
  "name": "Max Vax",
  "userId": "/users/maxvax",
  "callCountSuccess": 10,
  "callCountBlocked": 0,
  "callCountFailed": 0,
```

```
"callCountOther": 0,
"callCountTotal": 10,
"bandwidth": 250,
"cacheHitCount": 0,
"cacheMissCount": 0,
"valueCacheHitCount": 0,
"valueCacheMissCount": 0,
"apiTimeAvg": 323.81811000000005,
"apiTimeMin": 0.23670000000000002,
"apiTimeMax": 3234.5856000000003,
"serviceTimeAvg": 0,
"serviceTimeMin": 0,
"serviceTimeMax": 0
}
```

Based on this report, you not only know how many digital assets a user has requested but also how the overall experience was by analyzing the number of failed requests and the average response time.

Azure Automation

Azure Automation allows – as the name suggests – to perform actions in your (non)-Azure environment such as automatically shutting down a VM every night at 10 pm, installing weekly updates to VMs, or triggering other necessary operations at a predefined time.

As an example, we used Azure Automation to take a backup of an Azure API Management instance once a day. Even though it is possible to deploy the API gateway in different regions and protect your APIs, products, etc. from loss because of an unlikely disaster, this feature is only available in the premium tier of Azure API Management. Having a backup of your Azure API Management inventory might be a good idea if you run only with one instance.

In this chapter, you will learn to connect an Azure Automation account to change a certain named value frequently in Azure API Management. Whenever we deployed an entirely new Azure Kubernetes Service (AKS) cluster for our backend web services – that is how we updated AKS – we had to re-route the traffic that was going to Azure API Management from the old AKS cluster to the new AKS cluster. We did this by changing the backend service URL in the global policy, which was dynamically set as a named value in Azure API Management. The change was performed automatically by a PowerShell runbook in Azure Automation. When the URL of AKS changed in our source code repository, the runbook in the Azure Automation account was triggered. It then changed the URL of the AKS cluster, which was set as a named value in Azure API Management.

Creating an Azure Automation Account

We start by creating an Azure Automation account from the Azure portal. An Azure Automation account serves as a container for runbooks and other assets to execute a job.

Click "Create a new resource" from the start page and search for **Automation**, then click "Create," as shown in Figure 17-15. Choose a name, subscription, resource group, and location. Furthermore, select "Yes" in the field for creating an "Azure Run As" account. This creates a service principal with the contributor role on the subscription level which gives you full access to all Azure resources within the same subscription. Read more about service principal in the Azure documentation.

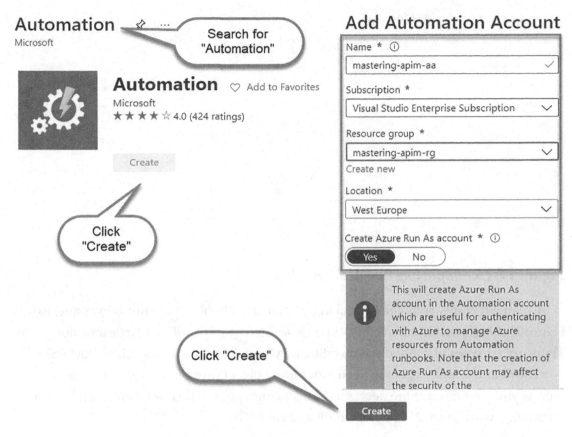

Figure 17-15. *Creating an Azure Automation account from the Azure portal*

To connect to your Azure account and to use the Azure PowerShell module for Azure API Management, you need to import two modules, *Az.Account* and *Az.ApiManagement*. You can do this under the **Modules** section in the left-hand menu of your Azure Automation account, as Figure 17-16 shows. Click "Browse gallery" and search for both modules to import them.

Figure 17-16. *Importing two Azure modules*

Create an empty runbook by clicking "Create a runbook" in the Runbook pane, as Figure 17-17 shows. Give it a name – I chose *mastering-apim-rb* – and a description. There are six types of runbooks: PowerShell, Python 2, Python 3, Graphical, PowerShell Workflow, and Graphical PowerShell Workflow. Select PowerShell as your runbook type as you already have the necessary skills to understand the PowerShell cmdlets for interacting with Azure API Management and click "Create."

Figure 17-17. *Creating an empty PowerShell runbook*

An editor for your PowerShell runbook opens where you will put your code for connecting to your Azure API Management instance. As Figure 17-18 shows, there is already listed your Azure resources connection with the name *AzureRunAsConnection*.

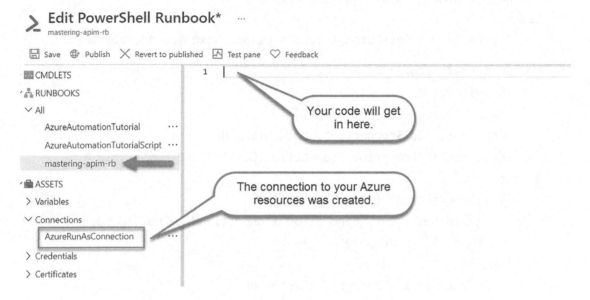

Figure 17-18. *PowerShell runbook editor*

Connecting to Azure API Management

Create a function `setupConnection` where you put your code for establishing a connection to your Azure account. Listing 17-2 demonstrates step by step how to implement this by using the internal PowerShell cmdlet `Get-AutomationConnection`. The cmdlet expects the name of your connection as the only parameter. It returns the service principal that was automatically created when you created an Automation account. The following Azure PowerShell cmdlet `Connect-AzAccount` connects to your Azure account as the name suggests. It requires three parameters that you get from your service principal, `TenantId`, `ApplicationId`, and `CertificateThumbprint`. I have put the code into a *try-catch* construct to make sure you get a proper error message in case your code does not work as expected. Finally, call your function `setupConnection`.

Listing 17-2. PowerShell function to connect to Azure API Management

```
function setupConnection {
    $connectionName = "AzureRunAsConnection"
    try {
        $connection = Get-AutomationConnection -Name $connectionName

        Connect-AzAccount `
        -ServicePrincipal `
        -TenantId $connection.TenantId `
        -ApplicationId $connection.ApplicationId `
        -CertificateThumbprint $connection.CertificateThumbprint
    } catch {
        if (!$connection) {
            $ErrorMessage = "Connection $connectionName not found."
            throw $ErrorMessage
        } else{
            Write-Error -Message $_.Exception
            throw $_.Exception
        }
    }
}

# Call the function to establish a connection
setupConnection
```

From here on, you can manage all your Azure resources within the same subscription. To demonstrate this, Listing 17-3 adds a new named value "test" to your Azure API Management instance. You understand the code already from previous chapters.

Listing 17-3. Creating a new named value from a runbook

```
$apimSubscriptionId = "b0e68700-2b10-4f92-858a-36d2a98748b8"
$apimServiceName = "mastering-apim"
$rg = "mastering-apim-rg"
```

```
Set-AzContext -Subscription $apimSubscriptionId
$context = New-AzApiManagementContext -ResourceGroupName $rg -ServiceName
$apimServiceName

New-AzApiManagementNamedValue -Context $context -NamedValueId "test" -Name
"test" -Value "value"
```

I hard coded the value for the named value at this point to simplify the example for you. In a production environment, you might want to get the value from the payload of a trigger. As mentioned before, when we change a property file for Azure API Management where we store all named values, the runbook gets automatically triggered. This happens because we synchronize the property file with an Azure App Configuration Service. Azure App Configuration is another Azure service for storing key/value pairs in plain text, almost like Azure Key Vault for encrypted values. Whenever a value changes in Azure App Configuration, an event is sent which the Azure Automation runbook listens to.

You learned in this section to use Azure Automation to perform actions in Azure API Management by connecting to your Azure account with an auto-generated service principal. To get a detailed introduction to Azure Automation, visit `https://docs.microsoft.com/en-us/azure/automation/automation-intro`.

Azure Logic Apps

With Azure Logic Apps, you create and run automated *workflows* that integrate backend services, data, but also on-premises systems. Logic Apps simplify the way that you can connect legacy and modern services no matter where they are located or with what technology they come.

A simple Logic App that I created some time ago is triggered by an HTTP request (step 1 in the workflow), reads a CSV file from a co-located drive (step 2), extracts all email addresses from this file (step3), and finally sends an invitation email to each email address (step 4). What I built was essentially a simple email distribution service by using Azure Logic Apps.

A more professional Logic App might include steps where several web APIs are called which run at different places and with different technologies, as Figure 17-19 shows.

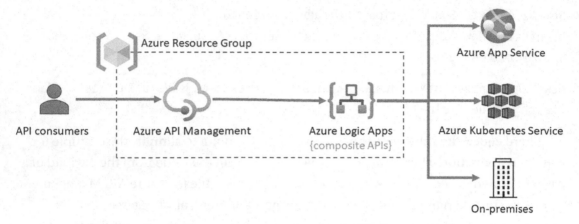

Figure 17-19. *Azure Logic Apps integrated with different technology stacks*

I was involved in a project where we developed several Azure Logic Apps that manage different aspects of managing incidents, creating Jira tickets, informing stakeholders, etc. We had one Logic App that was listening to events that were pushed from a monitoring system, in this case Dynatrace, and that orchestrated all steps in the chain of managing an ongoing incident; we called the Logic app *MASTER_INCIDENT_ HANDLER.* It created a Jira ticket where we kept the current status and actions being taken. The Logic App also created a Confluence page where all communication we had in a Slack channel was stored. It then posted the links of the pages to the Slack channel that we used as our main communication platform. Another Azure Logic App was triggered which was watching the Slack channel and stored all communication in a database but also updates the Confluence page at the same time. Both Azure Logic Apps used several web APIs such as the Dynatrace API, Confluence API, Jira API, and Slack API. Azure Logic Apps is a great PaaS service for orchestrating workflows.

In the following example, we combine two Azure Logic Apps into one API in Azure API Management. Both Logic Apps have an HTTP endpoint. The first Logic App lists customers, while the second Logic App creates new customers. We call the API for *Customer API,* as illustrated in Figure 17-20.

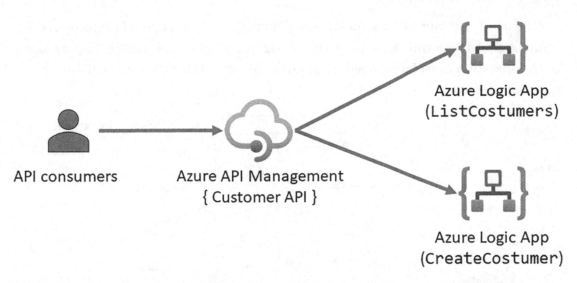

Figure 17-20. *Two Azure Logic Apps combined as one API*

When you can create an API from an Azure resource in the Azure portal such as from an *Azure Logic App*, it automatically suggests the name of the resource, in this case *ListCustomers*. You can change this directly in the form for creating the API as Figure 17-21 shows, or you can change the name later in the settings tab of the API. In this example, I changed the suggested *Display name* from *ListCustomers* to *Customer API* and set the context path (API URL suffix) to *customers*.

Create from Logic App

Basic	Full

*	Logic App	ListCostumers		Browse
*	Display name	Customer API ←		
*	Name	customer-api		
	API URL suffix	customers ←		

Base URL
```
https://mastering-apim.azure-api.net/customers
```

Create   Cancel

Figure 17-21. *Creating an API from an Azure Logic App*

The new Customer API has one API operation, the endpoint of the *ListCustomers* Azure Logic App. As you can see in Figure 17-22, some values such as the display name for the operation must be changed. You can do this by clicking the pencil in the upper-right corner.

Figure 17-22. *API operation of Azure Logic App*

As you see in Figure 17-23, the API operation name is *manual-invoke* and might be different from what we would expect. Change this to *ListCustomers* by changing the *Display name*. Also change the HTTP method from POST to GET, as well as the context-path from /manual/path/invoke to /customers.

Figure 17-23. *Setting correct values for an API operation*

As you already have the Customer API created with *ListCustomers* as its first API operation, you must add the second Azure Logic App *CreateCustomers* by creating a blank API operation. Open the *Frontend* dialog and set the right values accordingly:

- **Display name:** CreateCustomers

- **Name:** creatcustomers

- **URL:** POST as the HTTP method and customers as the context path

This API operation does not yet forward requests to the *CreateCustomers* Azure Logic App. To do this, click the pencil in the Backend section for the *HTTP(s) endpoint,* as shown in Figure 17-24.

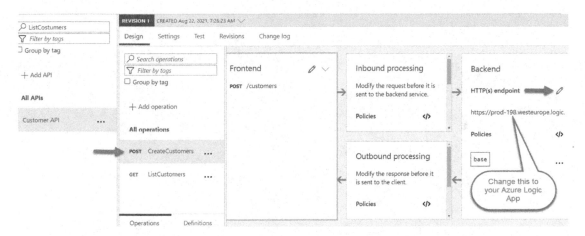

Figure 17-24. *Changing the backend URL for the Azure Logic App*

This opens a dialog where you can select an Azure resource. Browse to your Azure Logic App and click *Save.* The address that you see beneath the *HTTP(s) endpoint* changes to the Azure resource that you selected.

You can change most settings for an API and API operation also with the Azure CLI, PowerShell, or REST. However, importing an Azure Logic App is only possible from the Azure portal. To automate the process of updating the API, you need to create an open API definition file for the targeted Azure Logic apps that you can import with the PowerShell cmdlet `Import-AzApiManagementApi`.

Summary

In this chapter, you learned to set up and configure Azure API Management for some typical tasks that administrators of Azure API Management often are responsible for. You learned what you can do to set up and configure your instance for high availability but also to improve the overall performance so you can improve the experience of requesting digital assets. You learned also to generate reports that you can use to monetize your APIs. Finally, I taught you to connect Azure API Management and Azure Logic Apps.

Index

A

Add-AzApiManagementApiToProduct cmdlet, 53

Amazon Web Service (AWS), 162

Application Insights, 228–231

Application repositories, 127, 128

ARM templates, 29, 38, 127, 147, 154, 160, 162

Azure Kubernetes Service (AKS), 103

Authentication
- HTTP, 199, 200
  - API demo, 201
  - inbound operation, 202
  - Nginx, 200
- OAuth 2.0, 202
  - API, 210
  - Backend App, 203–205
  - Client App, 206, 207
  - configuration, 209
  - endpoints, 208
  - JWT, 212–214
  - test and validate, 212

az apim api command, 44

az apim api operation update command, 43

az group create command, 47

Azure API management
- account, 3
- add API, 7–9
- Azure portal, 29
- CLI, 29
- definition, 27

development portal, 31, 32

drawback, 78

gateway, 32, 33

Microsoft credentials, 3

networking, 28

PowerShell, 30

provision, 4–6

test API
- command line, 11
- portal, 9, 10
- Studio code, 9

URL, 91

Azure Automation, 249
- connect API, 253, 254
- create, 250–252

Azure Bicep, API deployment, 154–156

Azure Kubernetes Service (AKS), 15, 28, 123, 182–185, 249

Azure portal
- developing policies, 133
- inbound policies, 134
- policy code snippets, 135, 136
- policy configuration, 135
- policy editor, 136
- query parameters, 135
- ready-to-use policies, 133, 134

Azure PowerShell, 44, 220–223, 238

Azure Resource Manager templates (ARM templates), 147
- API deployment, 148
- Azure CLI, 154
- Azure Storage Account, 151

Printed in the United States
by Baker & Taylor Publisher Services